WHO'S WHO IN
SHAKESPEARE

Queen Katharine: "Lord Cardinal to you I speak"

Stratford- 1902.   Ellen Terry: Henry VIII.
Upon-Avon =

WHO'S WHO IN
SHAKESPEARE

WENDY NELSON-CAVE

CHARTWELL
BOOKS, INC.

Published by
BOOK SALES INC
114 Northfield Avenue
Raritan Center
Edison, NJ 08818

Produced by
Brompton Books Corp.
15 Sherwood Place
Greenwich, CT 06830

ISBN 0-7858-0222-3

Printed in China

PAGE 1 Portrait of William
Shakespeare, attributed to John Taylor,
c.1610.

PAGE 2 (clockwise from top left)
Edwin Booth as Iago; Ellen Terry as
Katharine of Aragon, poster by Pamela
Coleman Smith; Kenneth Branagh as
Laertes; Jeremy Irons as Richard II.

CONTENTS

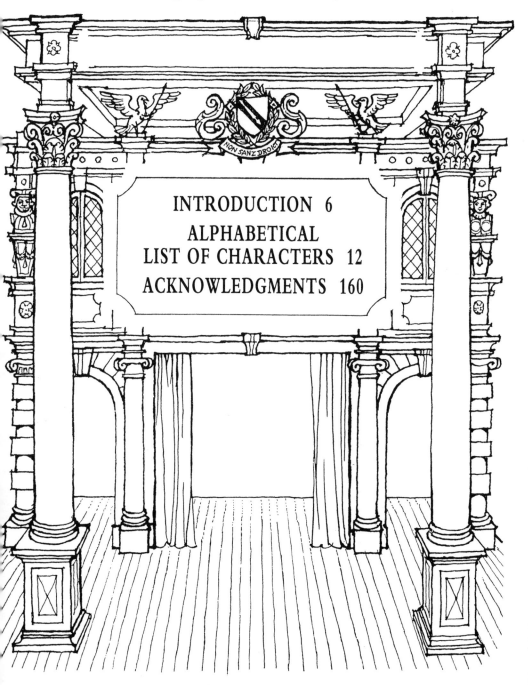

INTRODUCTION

The world of Shakespearean performance will come full circle when the newly rebuilt Globe Theatre opens on London's South Bank, adjacent to the site of the original playhouse. This new theatre will be as similar in design to the original as scholarly research can make it, and will replicate as closely as possible to production techniques of Shakespeare's own day. The new Globe represents a triumph for the late Sam Wanamaker, American actor, director and visionary, who led the crusade to rebuild it. Like the original, the new theatre will be an open-air, seasonal building, in which the audience will be seated close to the actors and on three sides of the stage. Some promenaders will take the place of the former 'groundlings', and tiered balconies will look down on the stage. The opening lines of *Henry V* (*c.* 1599), spoken by Chorus, exactly describe the Globe.

Can this cock-pit hold
The vasty fields of France? Or may we cram
Within this wooden O the very casques
That did affright the air at Agincourt?
O pardon: since a crooked figure may
Attest in little place a million,
And let us, ciphers to this great account,
On your imaginary forces work.

It is intended that many performances will be matinées, acted in natural daylight, and when evening performances require electric light, this will be uniformly spread over actors and audience and will avoid excessive effects. Little or no mechanical sound amplification is planned, as a guiding

The building of the new Globe Theatre, Southwark, 1994.

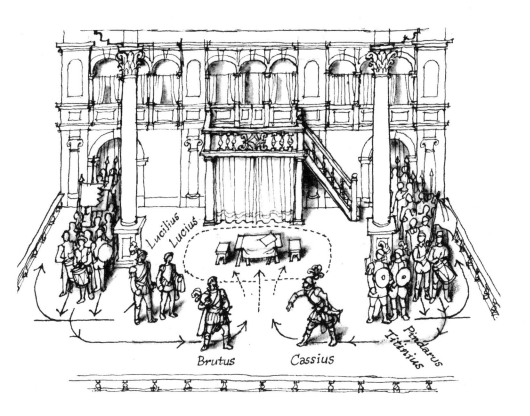

Lucilius
Lucius
Brutus
Cassius
Pindarus
Titinius

principle of the project is to put primary emphasis on the actor's speech and projection. Live music will be used where appropriate. It is even intended to stage some all-male productions, as was the rule in the original Globe. Above all, there will be a return to the Elizabethan idea that the audience comes first and foremost to hear the play, rather than see it.

The earliest recorded performances of the plays of William Shakespeare (1564-1616) were staged at the Rose Theatre in 1592, an earlier building than the Globe, on a nearby site. In that year we know that *Henry VI Part I* and *Titus Andronicus* were presented at the Rose. This makes the recent rediscovery of the ruins of the Rose, soon followed by the rediscovery of the Globe foundations, all the more evocative. Regrettably, excavation of the two theatres was not completed, due to pressure of time, and work has now ceased for an indefinite period. The new theatre reflects the knowledge gathered

ABOVE *Julius Caesar* in performance. BELOW Sam Wanamaker watching *The Merry Wives of Windsor*, 1993.

from these excavations, and stands a stone's throw from the hallowed ruins.

Elizabethan theatres ran on a repertory system. The daily change of programme was a great challenge to the actors, but this system was undoubtedly instrumental in achieving the high standard of acting which was a feature of the Globe and other companies. The Globe was opened in 1599, in the final years of Elizabeth I's reign, by a partnership consisting of Richard and Cuthbert Burbage (the latter not an actor), William Shakespeare, John Heminge, Henry Condell, Will Kempe, Augustine Phillips and Thomas Pope. The original Globe burned down only 14 years later in 1613, when a cannon was fired as part of a performance of *Henry VIII* and a spark set the thatched roof on fire. Despite this sinister precedent, the new theatre will have a thatched roof, although modern fire precautions have been incorporated. Shakespeare was probably in retirement at Stratford when the play which he had co-authored with John Fletcher caused the destruction of the theatre. Within a year the Globe was rebuilt and reopened, and operated until the Puritans closed the London theatres in 1642. Two years later the second Globe was pulled down.

At the original Globe, a strong company headed by Richard Burbage gave the first performances of most of the plays of Shakespeare, as well as works by other contemporary playwrights. Burbage was the first truly great English actor, and it is relatively certain that he created Richard III, Hamlet, Malvolio, Othello and Lear; his versatility must have been immense.

In 1660, at the time of the restoration of the monarchy, Charles II put a high priority on re-establishing drama. Two companies were founded by royal charter, the King's Men and the Duke's Men. These companies were the origins of the theatres royal at Drury Lane and Covent Garden, and dominated the scene for generations. At the Restoration, theatre moved from Southwark to the West End and became an indoors institution with

Portrait of Richard Burbage.

performances at night. Audiences had shrunk during the eighteen-year closure, and a gradual rebuilding of this base brought with it many changes.

As regards Shakespeare in performance, the most important change was the introduction of actresses. Although the Queen and nobly-born ladies had performed in the Stuart court masques, it was not until 1660 that the first professional actresses appeared in the public theatres. Two years later a royal warrant was issued decreeing that women, rather than boy actors, must now by law enact all female parts. Would that Shakespeare could have lived to see what an improvement in verisimilitude this made in the performance of his plays!

Although it is not possible to say with certainty who was the first actress on the English stage, it is known that on 8th December 1660 a woman acted Desdemona in a production of *Othello* by the King's Company, under the management of Thomas Killigrew. The other two female parts were still taken by males, although Killigrew had taken on four actresses. At the same time his rival, Sir William Davenant (said to be Shakespeare's godson), hired six actresses for the Duke's Company.

Davenant was responsible for the introduction in the public theatre of movable and changeable scenery behind a proscenium arch, innovations with which he was familiar from his earlier work on the Stuart masques with the designer Inigo Jones. Jones had introduced these to England as a result of his studies in Italy, and had incorporated them into his designs for Stuart masques. Although Restoration theatre design did retain the wide forestage of the Elizabethans, and the two proscenium arch doors to left and right may have been a carry-over from the doors at the back of the Elizabethan stage, nevertheless stage features and procedures were now very different. This affected acting styles, and a new emphasis on stage spectacle began to make itself felt. The repertory system, however, remained a constant.

The next great actor after Burbage was Thomas Betterton, whose long career began in 1660. Betterton, too, was outstanding in both tragedy and comedy, his Hamlet and Sir Toby Belch being particularly admired. Betterton adapted the plays of Shakespeare to suit the tastes of the times, beginning a long tradition of tampering with the text. He and his actress-wife, Mary Sanderson, were a great encouragement to younger players and their protegée, Anne Bracegirdle, rose to be one of the most outstanding actresses in English history. She played the lighter range of Shakespearean heroines, such as Cordelia, Desdemona, Ophelia and Portia. Bracegirdle's friend, Elizabeth Barry, surpassed her, however, and was especially noted as Lady Macbeth and Queen Katharine. The trio of Betterton, Bracegirdle and Barry were the cornerstones of Restoration acting.

Drastic revisions of the plays of Shakespeare continued to be the norm from the late seventeenth until the early twentieth century. Even David Garrick, the greatest actor of the eighteenth century and a particular admirer of the Bard, was fairly free with cuts and rewrites. The eighteenth century in England has been justly called 'the age of Garrick'; his vast influence was felt not only in the theatre but in the visual arts. He made his formal London debut in 1741, when he electrified the town with his new, naturalistic interpretation of Richard III, although King Lear was considered his greatest character. During his 29-year tenure as actor-manager at Drury Lane, Garrick produced 24 plays by Shakespeare and personally acted in 19.

Over the years Garrick surrounded himself with an excellent acting company. Notable actresses included Hannah Pritchard, who acted Lady Macbeth opposite Garrick's Macbeth for twenty years; he dropped *Macbeth* from his repertoire when she died in 1768. A few months before his retirement, Garrick introduced Sarah Siddons on to the London stage, and acted Richard III to her Lady Anne. Her six months with

Diana, a costume sketch by Inigo Jones.

Garrick was in fact a failure, but was probably the catalyst which enabled her, in the fullness of time, to become the greatest actress in English history.

Roughly coincident with the early career of Garrick was the birth of American theatre, in Virginia. The first important Shakespeareans in America were the Hallams, a family of English actors. Their performance of *The Merchant of Venice* is recorded in 1752 at Williamsburg, Virginia, where a theatre had been established about 20 years earlier. The Hallams performed *Richard III* in New York in 1753, and their operations covered a 50-year span in the United States. The popularity of Shakespeare continued on the American stage during the nineteenth century; the greatest American Shakespearean was Edwin Booth, whose record-breaking run of 100 nights as Hamlet was concluded during the Civil War.

Booth was later to appear with Henry Irving and Ellen Terry at the Lyceum in London, where the two men alternated the roles of Othello and Iago. Irving's management of the Lyceum with Ellen Terry, may be compared with the earlier and equally durable partnership of Mrs Siddons and her brother, John Philip Kemble. Mrs Siddons is accepted as the greatest Lady Macbeth ever, and Kemble was especially noted as Hamlet and Coriolanus. Irving and Terry's most famous production was *The Merchant of*

Contemporary illustration of *Titus Andronicus*, attributed to Henry Peacham, 1594.

Venice, which was seen not only in the British Isles but in the United States and Canada; their last appearance as Shylock and Portia was in 1902.

Irving was the first actor to be knighted, and this precedent was to set the stage for many titled actors, with the award of the highest honour, the Order of Merit to Lord Laurence Olivier. The works of Shakespeare have been the cornerstone of the careers of many actors aspiring to the highest reputation. Although the American Shakespearean tradition declined after John Barrymore's *Hamlet* in 1922, which broke Booth's record, it has been kept alive by festivals, films and university productions.

Perhaps the most important development in Shakespearean performance since the introduction of actresses in 1660, was the return to the principle of presenting the texts as Shakespeare wrote them. William Poel (1852-1934) was a pioneering advocate of productions which respected the purity of the text, and attempted to return to the original methods of presentation. This was taken up by actor-manager and critic Harley Granville-Barker in the early twentieth century, but it was not until the post-war years that these ideas were generally accepted.

A theatre was established at Stratford-upon-Avon, Shakespeare's birthplace, in 1879 and opened on the author's birthday, 23rd April. Its history has been varied, but in 1960 it changed its name to the Royal Shakespeare Company, having gradually evolved into the celebrated repertory company which is known around the world today, and which is the chief guardian of the works of Shakespeare in performance. It is the policy of the Royal Shakespeare Company to present all 37 of the canonical plays within a reasonable length of time, although obviously the more popular plays appear more often. A thirty-eighth play, *The Two Noble Kinsmen*, was chosen to open the new Swan Theatre in 1986. Many stars of the first rank, from Ellen Terry to Laurence Olivier, have acted at Stratford.

Seasonal Shakespeare festivals are found not only at Stratford, but in the USA and Canada. Films, musical comedies, radio and television performances based on Shakespeare, and university productions, have expanded the audience for the author's work. As new mediums and new audiences join the long history of Shakespeare in performance, developments at the new Globe Theatre, which will take us back to the roots, will be of immense interest to all lovers of Shakespeare. This will come to fruition in the reign of Elizabeth II, 396 years after the first Globe opened under Elizabeth I. As the Globe's patron, HRH Prince Philip, has rightly said: 'This project will give future generations of all lands a new and unique dimension in which to savour the genius of William Shakespeare'.

A Note on the Text

This volume contains entries for all the characters in those plays by Shakespeare which John Heminge and Henry Condell, the first editors, included in the First Folio (1623). These 36 works included *Henry VIII* (1613), a collaboration between Shakespeare and John Fletcher (1579-1625), but did not include *Pericles, Prince of Tyre* (*c*.1609). The reason for the omission may have been that Heminge and Condell knew that *Pericles* was not entirely by their friend, but were uncertain of the details of collaboration. The First Folio also excluded *The Two Noblemen Kinsmen*, probably written *c*.1613, which was first published in 1634 as 'by the memorable worthies of their time, Mr John Fletcher and Mr William Shakespeare'. Although this was 28 years after the death of Shakespeare, there is no real reason to disbelieve the ascription, as numerous plays were printed posthumously. It is felt that the present volume would be most useful to the reader if this play were likewise included here. The result is a very complete dictionary of the *dramatis personae* of Shakespeare.

A

Aaron

The main villain in Shakespeare's first tragedy, *Titus Andronicus* (*c*.1594), Aaron, a Moor, is a rare example, with Othello, of a black character in the author's works. He is the lover of Tamora, Queen of the Goths, and is the means of her revenge on Titus, who has allowed her son to be killed. Aaron plans the hideous rape which the two sons of Tamora carry out on Lavinia, Titus's daughter, whose tongue is cut out and her hands amputated to prevent her identifying her attackers. Aaron revels in his evil, and his character in this revenge tragedy foreshadows the playwright's later villains, Richard III and Iago. He is the stock character in drama known as a 'machiavel,' one who is flamboyant in his villainy.

Ira Aldridge as an epoch-making Aaron.

Abbess, The

Also known as Emilia, this matronly lady figures in Shakespeare's shortest play, *The Comedy of Errors* (*c*.1594). She only appears in the final scene, as the long-lost wife of Egeon and mother of his identical twin sons, Antipholus of Ephesus and Antipholus of Syracuse, the young heroes. The Abbess of Ephesus functions structurally almost as a '*deus ex machina*', in that her purpose is to tie up the loose ends of a plot which can only be disentangled by the introduction of a late character. She invites all to a feast, and her role as a symbol of Christian mercy mitigates the stern justice of the Duke of Ephesus who had condemned her hapless husband, Egeon.

Abergavenny, George Neville, Lord

Historical figure and minor character in the history play *Henry VIII* (1613), a late collaboration between Shakespeare and John Fletcher. Abergavenny joins his father-in-law, the Duke of Buckingham, and the Duke of Norfolk in opposing Cardinal Wolsey, but they are arrested for treason.

Abhorson

One of many characters in Shakespeare who is given a symbolic name to indicate his chief function or suggest his personality, Abhorson is an executioner in the dark comedy *Measure For Measure* (1604). He figures in the sub-plot, training the pimp, Pompey, as his assistant. They are supposed to execute Barnardine, a dissolute felon, but the prisoner refuses to co-operate.

Abraham

A minor servant of Romeo's father in *Romeo and Juliet* (1597), Abraham joins in the altercation with the servants of Juliet's family.

Achilles

A legendary figure whom Shakespeare takes from Homer's *Iliad* and incorporates into *Troilus and Cressida* (*c*.1603). Achilles, a leading character in the play, is a great Greek warrior, but at first refuses to fight in the Trojan War, and is shown as rude and insubordinate. Finally, in Act V, he does fight to avenge the death of his friend Patroclus. The pride of Achilles, which is a principal theme in Homer, is also central to Shakespeare's conception. Achilles claims the honour of having defeated the heroic Trojan Hector, but he has merely incited his followers to butcher his rival.

Adam

The aged servant of Orlando, the hero of *As You Like It* (1600), Adam was traditionally said to have been acted by Shakespeare himself. The character is derived from Shakespeare's source, *Rosalynde*, by Thomas Lodge, and is in the tradition of the old loyal servant. Adam offers his savings to help Orlando flee to the Forest of Arden, but the old man nearly dies of exhaustion and starvation on the journey. In Act II Orlando appears with Adam on his back, and their entry falls strategically after the famous 'Seven Ages of Man' speech has been delivered by Jacques. The sight of Adam poignantly punctuates the final line, 'Sans teeth, sans eyes, sans taste, sans everything', especially given his symbolic name, with its biblical overtones.

Adrian

Minor character in The Tempest (1611).

Adrian

A secondary character in Shakespeare's last Roman play, *Coriolanus* (*c*.1608), Adrian is a spy who obtains information for his tribe, the Volscians. He learns of the banishment of Coriolanus from Rome.

Adriana

A leading character in what is probably the author's first comedy, *The Comedy of Errors* (*c*.1594). Although the dramatist has followed his source, Plautus's *The Twin Meneachmi*, quite closely, he has expanded the importance of female characters and added a second set of twins. Adriana is the jealous but loving wife of Antipholus of Ephesus. She is an early example of the heroine as shrew, a role which Shakespeare developed more fully in Katherina and Beatrice in later comedies. Adriana was traditionally thought to be a portrait of Shakespeare's estranged wife, Anne Hathaway.

Aedile

Messengers in *Coriolanus* (*c*.1608), who are the subordinates of the Roman tribunes Sicinius and Brutus.

Aemilius

A messenger in *Titus Andronicus* (*c*.1594).

Aeneas

A legendary character from Homer's *Iliad* who is also found in *Troilus and Cressida* (*c*.1603), the author's third longest play. Shakespeare depicts Aeneas as a commander who represents the Trojan ideal of chivalry and acts as Hector's herald. The character is also central to Virgil's *Aeneid*.

Agamemnon

The leader of the Greek forces assailing Troy in *Troilus and Cressida* (*c*.1603). Agamemnon is not a particularly successful leader, and has difficulty in controlling his colleague Achilles. Agamemnon may have been a historical character who ruled in central Greece in the Bronze Age.

Zoe Wanamaker as Adriana with Jane Booker as Luciana, 1983.

Norman Forbes as Sir Andrew Aguecheek, 1932.

Agrippa, M. Vipsanius

A historical character found in *Antony and Cleopatra* (*c.*1608), one of the playwright's greatest tragedies, Agrippa is a follower of Octavius Caesar, and suggests the doomed marriage between Caesar's sister Octavia and Mark Antony. Agrippa commands Caesar's army, and is his close friend and right-hand man after the defeat of Antony and Cleopatra at Actium.

Aguecheek, Sir Andrew

A humorous secondary character in *Twelfth Night* (1602), who is duped by Sir Toby Belch into believing his niece, Countess Olivia, will entertain Sir Andrew's wooing. Sir Andrew is portrayed as ridiculous, both in appearance and manner; a shrivelled old man with stringy hair, he fancies himself an elegant wit and courtier. As a fighter, he follows the stock character line of the braggart soldier.

Ajax

A legendary character whom Shakespeare seems to have created from two characters of that name in the *Iliad*. In *Troilus and Cressida* (*c.*1603), Ajax is a variation on the braggart soldier, a stock figure in drama, which derives its type initially from Plautus's *Miles Gloriosus*. The comic, boasting soldier finds its fullest expression in Shakespeare's character, Sir John Falstaff. Ajax does, however, behave bravely when he faces the Trojan prince, Hector.

Alarbus

The eldest son of Tamora, Queen of the Goths, in *Titus Andronicus* (*c.*1594). Despite Tamora's pleas, Alarbus is killed by the sons of Titus, and this sets off the bloody cycle of events which inform this gruesome play.

Albany, Duke of

An important secondary character in Shakespeare's great tragedy *King Lear* (1608), Albany is the weak and ineffectual husband of Goneril, Lear's wicked eldest daughter. Albany discovers the full extent of her perfidy too late, but he aids the banished Lear by formally returning the King to power just before the old man dies. Albany, with Kent and Edgar, then shares power in Britain as the play closes. Although Albany lacks judgement, he is shown as well-meaning.

King Lear was first printed in a quarto of 1608, in which Albany is given the closing lines of the play, which summarise the moral and the tone of the tragedy:

The weight of this sad time we must obey;
Speak what we feel, not what we ought to say.
The oldest have borne most. We that are
     young
Shall never see so much, nor live so long.

This text is presumed to be as the author first conceived the play, but in the First Folio of 1623 and all subsequent editions, the final speech is given to Edgar, which may represent Shakespeare's own revision.

Alcibiades
(c.450-404 BC)
A historical personage used by Shakespeare as a major character in *Timon of Athens* (*c*.1604). Alcibiades is the only character, other than Timon, who is fully drawn, since the others are heavily symbolic or allegorical. He is found in the author's frequent source, Plutarch's *The Lives of the Noble Grecians and Romans*, where he is a more prominent figure. In the play, he is an Athenian general and a true friend to Timon, a nobleman who loses most of his friends when he runs out of money due to excessive generosity. Alcibiades is an active character who operates as a foil to the passive figure of the morose Timon.

Aldermen
Walk-ons found in *Henry VI Part 2* (*c*.1594), *Henry VI Part 3* (*c*.1595) and *Richard III* (*c*.1597).

Alençon, John, Duke of
This historical figure is a minor character in *Henry VI Part 1* (*c*.1592). He is a treacherous French nobleman leading the forces of Charles VII against the English.

Alexander
A very minor character who is a servant of Cressida in *Troilus and Cressida* (*c*.1603).

Alexas
A minor character, though historical, Alexas is a servant to the Queen of Egypt in *Antony and Cleopatra* (*c*.1608), but he deserts to Caesar after the defeat of the lovers in battle. Shakespeare found Alexas in Plutarch's *Lives*.

Alice
Plays a minor but amusing role in *Henry V* (*c*.1599). A matronly character, she is lady-in-waiting to the French princess, Katherine, to whom she gives a comical lesson in speaking English. This foreshadows the later scene in which King Henry attempts to woo Katherine in halting French.

Yvonne Coulette as Alice, 1975.

Aliena
Not a separate character, but the fictitious name which Celia adopts in *As You Like It* (1600) when she and Rosalind travel in disguise to the Forest of Arden.

Alonso, King of Naples

Found in the last play which Shakespeare wrote alone, *The Tempest* (1611), Alonso is the father of the young hero, Ferdinand. They are both among those shipwrecked on the enchanted island where the story takes place. Before the play opens, Alonso has deposed Prospero as rightful Duke of Milan and replaced him by Prospero's brother Antonio, but he later begs Prospero's pardon and is reconciled to him. Antonio and he surrender Milan and this, together with the marriage of Ferdinand and Prospero's daughter Miranda, incorporates Alonso into the play's theme of forgiveness and reconciliation.

Ambassador

Any of several walk-on characters in *Henry V* (*c.*1599) representing the French king.

Ambassador

A minor figure in *Hamlet* (*c.*1602), who functions as an emissary from England to the King of Denmark.

Ambassador

A minor representative of Antony in *Antony and Cleopatra* (*c.*1608). He is identified as the 'schoolmaster' to Antony's children by Cleopatra and his use as a messenger may signify that Antony has run out of followers. Plutarch confirms that Antony sent his schoolmaster to Octavius.

Amiens

A singer in the woodland court of Duke Senior in *As You Like It* (1600). Amiens is not particularly individualised, but his singing adds great atmosphere to the pastoral life in the forest:

Under the greenwood tree,
Who loves to lie with me . . .

Andromache

The virtuous and brave wife of the defeated Trojan, Hector, in *Troilus and Cressida* (*c.*1603).

Angelo

A minor figure in *The Comedy of Errors* (*c.*1594), Angelo is a goldsmith and the friend of Antipholus of Ephesus. He makes the necklace which causes some of the comic complications.

Angelo

A leading character in Shakespeare's 'problem play', *Measure For Measure* (1604), Angelo is appointed temporary deputy for the Duke of Vienna, who describes him thus:

. . . Lord Angelo is precise,
Stands at a guard with envy, scarce confesses
That his blood flows, or that his appetite
Is more to bread than stone . . .

The Duke is deceived, however, and Angelo abuses his power by sentencing Claudio to death for sleeping with his betrothed, Juliet, before their marriage. When the condemned man's sister, Isabella, comes to plead with Angelo for her brother's life, he is seized with lust for her. As she is a novice of the Poor

Clare order of nuns, Angelo's insistence that she must yield her virginity to him in order to save her brother is particularly repellent. His hypocrisy in condemning Claudio for the lesser sin is also at the heart of this complex play. But the play is not a tragedy, and a contrived happy ending is achieved in which the Duke forgives Angelo, but forces him to marry his abandoned fiancée, Mariana. The character of Angelo is an extremely sophisticated creation by Shakespeare, and his psychology is fully explored, although the play's solution is weak.

Angus, Gilchrist, Thane of
This historical character is used in a minor way in *Macbeth* (*c*.1606). Angus is a Scottish nobleman who is a follower of the worthy King Duncan, and who later joins the rebellion against the usurper, Macbeth.

Anne Boleyn, later Queen of England
(*c*.1507-1536)
A secondary character in Shakespeare's

ABOVE LEFT Michael Pennington as Angelo, with Sinead Cusack as Isabella, 1986.
ABOVE Violet Vanbrugh plays Anne Boleyn, 1892.

history play written with Fletcher, *Henry VIII* (1613). She is lady-in-waiting to Queen Katharine of Aragon, Henry's first wife, but upon his divorce, Anne becomes his second wife and Queen of England. The authors adhere closely to the known facts in this play, and indeed it was known in their day as *All Is True*, but they are at pains to keep the focus on Katharine, and they dissociate Anne from her predecessor's fall. Although Anne has a small speaking part, she is silent during her coronation and does not appear at all in the final scene where her daughter, the future Elizabeth I, is baptised.

Anne Neville, Lady, later Queen of England (1456-1485)

A secondary character in *Richard III* (*c.*1597), she at first appears as the widow of Edward, Prince of Wales and the daughter-in-law of the late Henry VI, both of whom Shakespeare alleges were murdered by Richard. Anne Neville was the daughter of the Earl of Warwick, the so-called 'kingmaker' and thus she was a political pawn. Shakespeare shows Richard wooing and winning Anne over the coffin of Henry VI, and takes considerable liberty with history in suggesting that Richard did not love his wife, and that he was was instrumental in her murder when she was no longer of use to him.

Antenor

A minor character in *Troilus and Cressida* (*c.*1603), Antenor is a Trojan warrior captured by the Greeks and exchanged for Cressida.

Antigonus

A secondary character in the late 'problem play' *The Winter's Tale* (1611), Antigonus is an old nobleman at the court of the jealous king, Leontes of Sicily. He defends the Queen against the unjust charge of adultery upon which the plot hinges. Leontes does not believe the baby born to the Queen is his, and orders Antigonus to abandon it in the wilderness. In so doing, Antigonus is the subject of the celebrated stage direction, 'exit, pursued by a bear.' Needless to say, that ends his role in the play.

Antiochus, King of Syria

A historical character in *Pericles, Prince of Tyre* (*c.*1609), a play partly by Shakespeare and partly by an unknown author or authors. Antiochus is depicted as an incestuous father whose daughter is courted by Pericles in his wanderings, although there is no historical evidence for incest. He is shown as a conventional villain in other respects, and his part is small.

Christopher Ravenscroft as Antonio with Ian McDiarmid as Shylock, 1984.

Antipholus of Ephesus, Antipholus of Syracuse

A pair of twins whom we meet as mature young men in *The Comedy of Errors* (*c.*1594), and who have been parted as infants in a shipwreck before the play opens. They have twin servants who are zany in the manner of ancient Roman comedy; the addition of a second set of twins is a change from Shakespeare's source, Plautus's *The Twin Meneachmi*. Antipholus of Ephesus is married, whereas his twin is not. Twins obviously create a casting problem on the stage, and a second set of twins compounds the problem, but in such a fast-moving and short farce, it usually works. Shakespeare uses twins again in *Twelfth Night* (1602); as the father of twins himself, he obviously saw the funny side of it.

Antonio

A walk-on character in the early comedy, *The Two Gentlemen of Verona* (*c.*1598), Antonio is the father of Proteus, one of the two gentlemen of the title.

Antonio

The title character in *The Merchant of Venice* (*c*.1598). An older man, his love for his young friend Bassanio leads Antonio to borrow money on his friend's behalf from the Jewish usurer Shylock, who hates Antonio. Bassanio has fallen in love with Portia, an heiress whom he cannot afford to woo without Antonio's help. Shylock, pretending to joke, requires a pound of Antonio's flesh should the debt be forfeit. Shortly after the marriage, Antonio's ships miscarry and he is unable to pay his debt, but the ingenuity of Portia saves his life. Antonio is a sentimental and moody man. Modern directors have often fallen back on a homosexual interpretation of his character in order to explain his motivations, but we are left with a character who is rather bland and passive.

Antonio

This charming old man is the brother to Leonato, Governor of Messina, in *Much Ado About Nothing* (*c*.1599), and uncle to Hero. He fleshes out the family in the story, but is otherwise a minor character.

Antonio

A minor character in *Twelfth Night* (1602), Antonio rescues Sebastian from the shipwreck which separates him from his twin sister, Viola, the play's heroine.

Antonio

Usurping Duke of Milan and one of the villainous characters in *The Tempest* (1611) who, before the play opens, have deposed his brother Prospero. Along with the others, Antonio is shipwrecked on the magic island where Prospero rules in exile.

Antony, Mark
(Marcus Antonius, *c*.82-30 BC)

One of the most colourful characters in ancient history, and one of the playwright's great creations. Antony has a leading role in two of Shakespeare's Roman history plays, *Julius Caesar* (1599) and *Antony and Cleopatra* (*c*.1608). In the former play, we meet Antony as a young soldier in his prime, who leads the forces opposing the assassins of his friend, Julius Caesar. In the later play, the older, world-weary Antony is a much more fully developed character. His obsession with Cleopatra, formerly the mistress of Julius Caesar, has led Antony to neglect his duties in Rome in favour of a luxurious life with her in Egypt. This leads to a fatal confrontation with the young Octavius Caesar, whose sister Octavia is married to Antony. Antony is much loved by his men, and is in every sense a larger-than-life personality. In both plays, Shakespeare has written some of his finest dialogue for this character. In *Julius Caesar* Antony gives a cunning funeral oration over the body of Caesar:

Friends, Romans, countrymen, lend me your ears.
I come to bury Caesar, not to praise him.
The evil that men do lives after them;
The good is oft interred with their bones.
So let it be with Caesar.

Antony's shame, humiliation and suicide, which are the consequence of his abandonment of Octavia and his adultery with Cleopatra, rendered *Antony and Cleopatra* uncongenial to audiences prior to the twentieth century, and even so recent an expert as George Bernard Shaw

Marlon Brando as Mark Antony, Greer Garson as Calpurnia in the classic film of *Julius Caesar*, 1953.

Laurence Olivier as Mark Antony with Vivien Leigh as Cleopatra, 1951.

considered its unsavoury subject matter unsuitable for tragedy. It is very difficult to raise such duplicitous lovers to the necessary level of self-awareness and exaltation to achieve the tragic catharsis.

No early performances are recorded, but it is presumed that Shakespeare's friend and leading man, Richard Burbage, created the role opposite a boy actor as Cleopatra. David Garrick attempted it in 1759 opposite Mary Ann Yates, in a mangled version of the text, but this was a failure and was withdrawn, never to be repeated by him. In 1813 John Philip Kemble attempted a conflation of Shakespeare with the John Dryden version entitled *All For Love* (1678), with Helen Faucit, which likewise failed. Not until 1849 was the text staged as the author wrote it, but this production, with Samuel Phelps, also failed. In 1905 Sir Frank Benson eschewed spectacle for a simple staging, and this tendency was continued when the Old Vic staged the play in 1922 with Edith Evans, who repeated Cleopatra in several later

productions. In New York the play had a very notable success in 1947, with Katherine Cornell and Godfrey Tearle, and in 1951 Broadway again gave a warm welcome to the play with Laurence Olivier and Vivien Leigh. The Oliviers had been seen in *Antony and Cleopatra* in London, on a double bill with Shaw's *Caesar and Cleopatra* (1901). Although many successful stagings have been seen since, Olivier must surely stand as the best impersonator since Richard Burbage of Mark Antony.

Apemantus
This character from *Timon of Athens* (*c*.1604) functions almost like a chorus, in that he provides a running commentary on the plot. He is an angry, misanthropic philosopher.

Apothecary
A minor but significant role in *Romeo and Juliet* (1597), this nameless man sells Romeo the fatal poison with which he kills himself, believing that Juliet is dead.

Apparitions

Supernatural figures who make a brief but emblematic appearance in *Macbeth* (1606). The apparitions are shown to Macbeth by the three witches, and the prophecies made by these spirits are borne out.

Archidamus

A follower of King Polixenes of Bohemia in *The Winter's Tale* (1611).

Arcite

One of the title characters in *The Two Noble Kinsmen*, now generally accepted as by Shakespeare and John Fletcher, probably written *c.*1613 but which first appeared in print in 1634. Arcite and his cousin Palamon are affectionate friends and chivalrous knights; they become prisoners of war in Athens and fall in love with the same woman, which destroys their friendship. The first known performance of this play since the seventeenth century was by the Old Vic in 1928, but it was chosen to open the new Swan Theatre at Stratford-on-Avon in 1986.

Ariel

This ageless sprite is the chief fairy attendant on the magician Prospero in *The Tempest* (1611). As his name suggests, Ariel is largely airborne. He is usually invisible to all but Prospero, although when he assumes fantastic guises he can be seen by others. He is cheerful, intelligent and embodies the concept of Good in the play.

Margaret Leighton as Ariel with Ralph Richardson as Prospero, 1952.

Michael Hordern plays Armado, 1978.

Armado, Don Adriano de
A pompous Spaniard in *Love's Labour's Lost* (*c.*1598)

Arragon, Prince of
One of three suitors to Portia in *The Merchant of Venice* (*c.*1598) who, according to her father's will, must make a choice from three caskets of gold, silver and lead before their suit may continue. His choice of silver is wrong, and thus he loses her hand. Although his is a small role, Arragon is important to the plot, and his somewhat caricatured Spanish personality adds a touch of comedy.

Artemidorus
Historical character who is an ally of Caesar's in *Julius Caesar* (1599).

Artesius
A minor character in *The Two Noble Kinsmen* (*c.*1613) by Shakespeare and John Fletcher. He is an officer of Theseus, Duke of Athens, with whose sister-in-law the two young kinsmen are in love.

Arthur, Prince of England (1187-1203)
A historical figure, Arthur's claim to the English crown has been usurped as *King John* (*c.*1595) opens. He is the nephew and victim of the King, but his cause is supported by King Philip of France and the Archduke of Austria, who go to war with England. The death of Arthur provokes a rebellion by John's nobles.

Arviragus
One of the kidnapped sons of the King in *Cymbeline* (1611). Although not a history play, the author derives some of his material from Holinshed's *Chronicles*. Arviragus, known as Cadwal, has been raised with his brother in the wilds of Wales by an old hermit. When the Romans invade Britain, the brothers distinguish themselves and are subsequently reunited with their father, King Cymbeline.

Asnath
An evil spirit in Part 2 of *Henry VI* (*c.*1594), this minor character is summoned up by the witch, Margery Jourdain. Shakespeare is thought to have intended his name as an anagram of 'Sathan', the old spelling of Satan.

Audrey
A bucolic goatherd whom Touchstone meets in the Forest of Arden in *As You Like It* (1600), and intends to marry. Although a small role, Audrey is a well-drawn comic character who is used by the author, together with the other rustic lovers, Silvius and Phebe, to parody the pastoral tradition.

Aufidius, Tullus
A legendary character in *Coriolanus* (*c.*1608), who is of major importance as

Mirianne Caldwell as Audrey with Courtice Pounds as Touchstone.

the rival of the hero. He is the leader of the Volscians, and having frequently been defeated by Coriolanus, he at last succeeds in killing him. In some ways an admirable warrior, Aufidius is shown as corrupted by his obsession with defeating his rival; Shakespeare has greatly expanded the character as in Plutarch.

Aumerle, Edward, Duke of
Historical character found in *Richard II* (1597), a flattering, hypocritical courtier of Richard's. He also appears as a very minor figure in *Henry V* (c.1599), having inherited the title Duke of York.

Austria, Limoges, Archduke of
Shakespeare conflated two historical figures in creating this character for *King John* (c.1595). He depicts Austria as a supporter of the young Prince Arthur, claimant to the English throne.

Autolycus
A rascal in *The Winter's Tale* (1611) who wanders about Bohemia in the second part of this tragi-comedy, singing and bragging about his career as a thief. He describes himself as a 'snapper-up of unconsidered trifles', and adds atmosphere to the lighter part of the play.

Auvergne, Countess of
Minor character, a French noblewoman, in *Henry VI Part 1* (c.1592).

B

Bagot, Sir John
Historical character found in *Richard II* (c.1597), who together with his colleagues Henry Greene and John Bushy, is a follower of Richard. When Henry Bolingbroke defeats the King, their position becomes precarious, and Bushy and Greene are executed. Bagot, however, joins Richard in Ireland, returns to Westminster Abbey to accuse Aumerle of the murder of Thomas, Duke of Gloucester, but subsequently disappears from the play.

Balthasar
A merchant, a minor character in *The Comedy of Errors* (c.1594) who is a friend of Antipholus of Ephesus.

Balthasar
Has a small role in *Romeo and Juliet* (1597), but his moments on the stage are telling. He brings Romeo the erroneous news that Juliet is dead, thus causing the final phase of the tragedy. He accompanies Romeo to Juliet's tomb, but is sent away with a letter for Romeo's father. At the end this letter helps to explain to the grieving parents the circumstances of the lovers' death.

Balthasar
A servant in *The Merchant of Venice* (c.1598) who is sent by Portia with a letter to her cousin, requesting a disguise as a lawyer for Antonio's trial. She later takes the name of Balthasar as part of her disguise.

Balthasar
Although a minor character, his presence adds greatly to the atmosphere of the high comedy, *Much Ado About Nothing* (c.1599). He is a musician and singer, attendant on Don Pedro, Prince of Arragon. His love song, 'Sigh no more, ladies,' and his later lament sung at Hero's tomb, help to effect the change of mood which is a difficult feature of this play.

Bandit
Any one of three minor characters who are thieves in *Timon of Athens* (c.1604). They are cited as thieves in many editions, but called '*banditti*' in the stage direction.

Banquo
This major character in *Macbeth* (1606) is taken from Shakespeare's source, Holinshed's *Chronicles*. Banquo and Macbeth are Scottish thanes and make their first appearance together in the play as comrades-in-arms. Encountering three witches on the heath, their friendship

begins to deteriorate as a result of the differing prophecies which these hags give to them. Macbeth, they predict, will be King of Scotland, but Banquo's heirs will rule. Shakespeare, and perhaps more importantly his patron, James I, believed Banquo to be the ancestor of the Stuart line. Thus his role, in a play which seems to have been designed to please King James, was crucial. Modern scholarship finds no trace of Banquo as a historical character.

In the play, Macbeth orders the murder of Banquo and his young son Fleance, in order to prevent the witches' prophecy coming true. Having achieved the crown by his murder of King Duncan, Macbeth feels it will be but a hollow victory if his own heirs do not succeed. Although Macbeth's assassins succeed in killing Banquo, however, Fleance escapes. In one of Shakespeare's great theatrical moments, the Ghost of Banquo appears to Macbeth at a banquet and this scene is the turning point in the tragedy. Although the Ghost is invisible to everyone except Macbeth, Mrs Siddons, the greatest of all Lady Macbeths, played the banquet scene in the eighteenth century as if she too saw the Ghost.

Banquo is portrayed as a decent and honourable nobleman, whose response to the witches is in sharp contrast to the evil ambition of Macbeth. He warns Macbeth that 'ofttimes, to win us to our harm, the instruments of darkness tell us truths.' His imperviousness to their evil emphasises Macbeth's lack of resistance. The virtue of Banquo could be seen as a compliment to King James I.

Baptista

This appealingly comic father in *The Taming of the Shrew* (c.1594) is utterly unable to deal with his elder daughter, Katharina. He is frequently the butt of her wild outbursts of temper, which are the spring of the plot in Shakespeare's early farce. Baptista is firm on one point, however; he will not allow his younger daughter, Bianca, to wed until he can find a husband for Katharina. His character shows no development beyond his concern to get his daughters married.

Bardolph

One of Shakespeare's well-observed rustics, Bardolph appears in *Henry IV Parts 1 and 2* (1598/1600), in a medieval context, and in his farce *The Merry Wives of Windsor* (c.1597), in an Elizabethan setting. He is a drinking companion and follower of the fat knight, Sir John Falstaff, one of Shakespeare's greatest comic creations. Bardolph joins Falstaff in a highway robbery, and receives bribes on Falstaff's behalf from men wishing to avoid conscription into the King's army. In *Henry V* (1599) Bardolph is himself a soldier in the army, but is executed on the King's orders for stealing a chalice from a French church. Given that the King, in his wilder days as Prince of Wales, counted Bardolph a friend, his order to hang him for a religious crime strongly underlines the maturing of Henry's character. Bardolph is less important in *Merry Wives*, but he retains his characteristic red nose and his diseased facial complexion.

Alfred Brydone as Baptista.

Bardolph, Lord Thomas

A historical figure who appears in *Henry IV Part 2* (1600) as a follower of the Earl of Northumberland and a rebel against King Henry. He is referred to as Lord Bardolph to distinguish him from the comic, rustic Bardolph.

Barnardine

A minor figure in *Measure For Measure* (1604), who is a condemned felon, but is given an undeserved pardon by the Duke at the end, which strengthens the theme of reconciliation. Barnardine is comic in his drunkenness, and in his stubborn refusal to be executed.

Bartholomew

A page in the induction scene which opens *The Taming of the Shrew* (c.1594). He dresses as a lady in this curious introduction to the play proper.

Bassanio

The romantic male lead in *The Merchant of Venice* (c.1598) who has fallen in love with a rich heiress, Portia, whom he cannot afford to woo. He accepts a fatal loan from his friend, Antonio, the merchant of the title. Antonio in turn must borrow from the Jewish usurer, Shylock, in order to supply Bassanio. Shylock's bond requires a pound of Antonio's flesh should the debt be forfeit. Bassanio leaves Venice for Portia's estate, where he makes his choice of the three caskets of gold, silver and lead, as set down in the will of Portia's father. He makes the correct choice of lead, which was seen as a conventional indication of unselfish love. Although Bassanio is the hero of *The Merchant of Venice*, his story is not as compelling as that of Portia and her confrontation with Shylock. Bassanio is unconvincing as an ardent lover; he is bland, selfish and something of a fortune-hunter.

Basset

A minor character in *Henry VI Part 1* (c.1592), Basset is a supporter of the Duke of Somerset.

Jonathan Hyde plays Bassanio to Sinead Cusack's Portia, 1981.

Bassianus

Brother to the Emperor Saturninus in *Titus Andronicus* (c.1594). Bassianus is betrothed to Titus's daughter Lavinia and is outraged when Titus promises her instead to Saturninus. He is the first victim of the plots of the villain, Aaron, and Titus's sons are falsely accused of his murder.

Bastard, The, Philip Faulconbridge

A character in the early history play *King John* (c.1595) and John's nephew. The Bastard, although a fictional character, is the most prominent person in the play, a complicated character whose illegitimacy parallels the king's status as usurper. He rises while John falls, and is the first to acknowledge Henry as the new King.

Bastard of Orleans, The, Jean Dunois

Historical figure in *Henry VI Part 1* (*c*.1592). Dunois is one of the leaders of the French army and is depicted as a braggart soldier, although in reality he was one of the leading soldiers of the fifteenth century.

Bates, John

A typical English soldier whose minor characterisation in *Henry V* (*c*.1599) is important as depicting the morale of the King's army on the eve of the Battle of Agincourt. He figures in the brilliant scene where Henry walks incognito among his men.

Bavian

A minor character in *The Two Noble Kinsmen* (*c*.1613), a play sometimes placed among the apocrypha of Shakespeare, as of dubious authenticity. The character performs dressed as a baboon in an entertainment for Duke Theseus of Athens, and in that guise speaks only two words.

Bawd

A minor character in *Pericles*, *Prince of Tyre* (*c*.1609), a play which is also sometimes included among the apocrypha, and was omitted from the first folio of 1623. The bawd keeps a brothel in Mytilene in which the virtuous heroine, Marina, is kept against her will.

Beadle

A minor character in *Henry VI Part 2* (*c*.1594), a constable of St Albans.

Beadle

Any one of several minor characters in *Henry IV Part 2* (1600).

Bear

A minor but sensational, character in *The Winter's Tale* (1611). The bear kills the old man, Antigonus, who has been forced by the King's decree to abandon the infant heroine, Perdita, in the wilderness. One of the author's most famous stage directions, 'Exit, pursued by a bear', refers to this scenario. Expert opinion has pondered whether the dramatist intended the use of a live bear, since it is known that there was a bear-baiting arena only a few doors from the Globe Theatre, where the Elizabethans paid to see dogs attack bears. Tame bears were known in seventeenth-century England, but they were always on a lead, which would be inconsistent with the stage action in *The Winter's Tale*. Probably Shakespeare used an actor in a bear costume.

Beatrice

The heroine in *Much Ado About Nothing* (*c*.1599) whose witty, acerbic tongue, and intelligent, loving nature, have made her one of Shakespeare's best-loved characters, and as such a difficult challenge for the actress. She could be considered a refinement on Katherina, 'the shrew'. At first Beatrice will have none of love, and she disparages the qualities of Benedict. The audience knows she loves him all along, however, and the wronging of her cousin, Hero, is the means to bring Beatrice and Benedict together. Her lively character is well described when she says of herself ' . . . a star danced, and under that was I born.'

ABOVE Susan Fleetwood as a recalcitrant
Beatrice, 1991.
BELOW Felicity Kendal as Beatrice with Alan
Bates as Benedict, 1989.

Much Ado was immediately popular
when new, and remained so throughout
the seventeenth century, mainly on the
strength of Beatrice and Benedict. In the

eighteenth century, David Garrick kept it
in the Drury Lane repertoire between
1748 and his retirement in 1776. But the
character of Beatrice was most closely
associated with two later actresses, Helen
Faucit and Ellen Terry, the latter now
regarded as the definitive Beatrice. In the
mid-nineteenth century, Beatrice was also
engagingly acted on the American stage,
first by Fanny Kemble, and later by Anna
Cora Mowatt. In the twentieth century, a
whole range of successful productions
have been seen, and *Much Ado* has also
been filmed five times, most recently
with Kenneth Branagh and Emma
Thompson.

Beaufort, Cardinal Henry (1374-1447)
Historical character who is found in
Henry VI Part 2 (*c*.1594), and as the
Bishop of Winchester in *Henry VI Part 1*
(*c*.1592). He is the great-uncle of the
young King Henry and a powerful and
unscrupulous secular lord, who later
seems to die of a bad conscience.

Beaumont
A French nobleman in *Henry V* (*c*.1599),
a minor character who appears but does
not speak.

Bedford, John Plantagenet, Duke of (1389-1435)
A historical figure who appears in *Henry
VI Part 1* (*c*.1592) and *Henry V* (*c*.1599),
Bedford is the younger brother of Henry
V and uncle of Henry VI, and also
appears as Prince John of Lancaster in
Henry IV Parts 1 and 2 (1598/1600). In the
first part of *Henry VI*, Bedford opens the
play memorably, mourning Henry V,
whose death has left him ruling as Regent
of France. He dies happily, after
witnessing the success of English forces at
Rouen. In *Henry V* he is a younger
member of the King's retinue.

Belarius
An old man in *Cymbeline* (1611), a
secondary character calling himself
Morgan, who has been unjustly exiled

from King Cymbeline's court many years before, and revenged himself by abducting the King's two infant sons, Guiderius and Arviragus. Having raised them in the wilds of Wales, Belarius helps the boys save the British army when the Romans invade. He is shown as a good man, unjustly persecuted, and is finally forgiven by Cymbeline. He has a comic habit of speaking in clichés and would have been seen as depicting the seventeenth-century English stereotype of the unsophisticated Welshman.

Belch, Sir Toby

An important character in *Twelfth Night* (1602), whose symbolic name alludes to his habit of getting drunk too often. He is the elderly uncle of one of the heroines, Countess Olivia, and together with his fellow conspirators, Sir Andrew Aguecheek, Maria and Fabian, represents the festive side of the play. Their trick on Olivia's puritanical steward, Malvolio, triumphs in the central comic episode in the play. This is encapsulated in Sir Toby's taunt to Malvolio, 'Dost thou think because thou art virtuous, there shall be no more cakes and ale?' In some ways, Sir Toby resembles another great comic knight, Sir John Falstaff, in that he enacts a variety of roles and exploits people. In spite of his unpleasant faults, Sir Toby is a symbol of joy in living. It is reported at the end that he has married Maria.

Benedict

The romantic male lead in *Much Ado About Nothing* (c.1599), Benedict of Padua is a lord in the entourage of Don Pedro, Prince of Arragon, with whom he has seen military service before the play opens. He is a likeable young man, but ridicules all women and rails against marriage. He is tricked by Don Pedro and Claudio into believing that Beatrice loves him, however, which brings out his own affection for her:

The world must be peopled. When I said I would die a batchelor, I did not think I should live till I were married. Here comes Beatrice.

Robert Atkins plays Sir Toby Belch in 1932.

By this day, she's a fair lady. I do spy some marks of love in her.

In the eighteenth century many considered Benedict the greatest role of David Garrick; among notable nineteenth-century interpreters were Charles Kemble and Henry Irving.

Benvolio

A secondary character in *Romeo and Juliet* (1597), who is the cousin and friend of Romeo.

Berkeley

A walk-on character in *Richard III* (c.1597), one of two gentlemen who accompany Lady Anne as she follows the corpse of her father-in-law, Henry VI.

Berkeley, Lord Thomas

Historical figure and minor character in *Richard II* (c.1597). Berkeley is an ally of the Duke of York.

Bernardo

One of two sentries who set the scene in the opening of *Hamlet* (c.1602), where the Ghost of Hamlet's father appears on the ramparts.

Berowne (Biron)

One of three young courtiers to the King of Navarre in *Love's Labour's Lost* (c.1598). When the King proposes to dedicate himself to scholarship, he requires his three gentlemen-in-waiting to

Michael Pennington as Berowne with Richard Griffiths as the King 1978.

sign an oath giving up revelry and the company of women for three years. Two sign willingly, but Berowne is against such extremes and points out that the Princess of France is due to arrive soon. Unlike the others, he is a fully rounded character who expounds one of the play's principle points, that love is superior to the pursuit of knowledge. His name was taken from a contemporary French Protestant general, the Duc de Biron, adviser to the real King of Navarre.

Berri, Jean of France, Duke of
Although a real person, Berri has a minor role in *Henry V* (*c.*1599). He is a silent follower of the French King.

Bertram
A young French nobleman who is an important figure in *All's Well That Ends Well* (*c.*1603). His unsatisfactory character is one of the reasons this play is known as a 'problem play.' Helena, the delightful heroine, loves Bertram but he does not return her passion. She resorts to the 'bed trick', substituting herself for another woman and thus inducing Bertram to father her child. He is a self-absorbed young man who does not deserve Helena, but Shakespeare is at pains to emphasise Bertram's youth by way of excusing his follies. He goes to the wars and the Duke of Florence appoints him a cavalry commander, but he has attempted the seduction of the virginal Diana,

unknowingly bedding Helena in her place, and maligns Diana's reputation. He is redeemed by the power of Helena's love, but the resolution is unconvincing.

Bevis, George
Follower of Jack Cade in *Henry VI Part 2* (*c.*1594).

Bianca
The younger sister of 'the shrew', Katherina, in *The Taming of the Shrew* (*c.*1594), Bianca bears the brunt of Katherina's jealousy in that she is more popular with their father and with suitors. The courtship of Bianca by Lucentio, Hortensio and Grumio forms the sub-plot of this comedy. At first she seems a demure foil for her very robust sister, but there are hints that Bianca has a mind of her own. At the final banquet, Petruchio and Katherina seem more likely to enjoy a happy marriage than Bianca and Lucentio.

Bianca
Courtesan and secondary character in *Othello* (1604), she becomes the lover of Michael Cassio once the garrison has moved to Cyprus. Not a common whore, she has her own house and considerable pride. Her concern for the wounded Cassio shows her as a caring person, and her jealousy of Cassio underlines the larger theme of Othello's jealousy of his wife, Desdemona. Bianca is wrongfully arrested at the instigation of Iago.

Alice Krige as an innocent Bianca, 1982.

Bigot, Lord Roger

Historical figure with a minor role in *King John* (*c*.1595). Bigot is one of the noblemen who, reacting to the death of the claimant to the throne, Prince Arthur, oppose King John and ally themselves with the French.

Biondello

A servant in *The Taming of the Shrew* (*c*.1594), who is a follower of Lucentio, the successful suitor to Bianca, and gives a comic account of the extraordinary clothes which Petruchio chooses to wear for his wedding to Katherina.

Bishop

One of two minor clergymen in *Richard III* (*c*.1597) who accompany Richard when he receives the Lord Mayor. Richard intends to convey the impression that he was busy with devotions; the 'bishops' are actually unscrupulous lower clergy whom Richard has summoned for the deception.

Blanche of Spain (1188-1252)

A historical but minor character in *King John* (*c*.1595), Blanche is John's niece. She marries the French Dauphin, but when hostilities break out between England and France, she is reduced to helplessness.

Blunt, Sir James

A minor functionary in *Richard III* (*c*.1597), who is a follower of Richmond, the future Henry VII and the victor of Bosworth Field.

Blunt, Sir John

A minor functionary in *Henry IV Part 2* (1600), who is an aide to the King's brother, Prince John of Lancaster.

Blunt, Sir Walter

Historical figure in *Henry IV Part 1* (1598). A respected adviser and emissary of King Henry, he is killed in the King's service at the end of the play.

Boatswain

A bit part in *The Tempest* (1611).

Bolingbroke, Henry, later Henry IV (1366-1413)

A major figure in *Richard II* (*c*.1597) and the two parts of *Henry IV* (1598/1600). Henry is the son of John of Gaunt, Duke of Lancaster, and the cousin of King Richard II. We first meet him as a leading character in *Richard II* where, in the opening scene, he is banished by his cousin. Subsequently, on the death of John of Gaunt, Bolingbroke's estates are confiscated by Richard. The stage is then set for a fatal confrontation between the two cousins, which results in the usurpation of the throne by Bolingbroke and the murder of Richard II. The dilemma posed in the play is that Bolingbroke is far better suited to be king, but Richard rules by divine right which, according to the thinking of the Middle Ages, was inviolable. Bolingbroke, now Henry IV, does not personally order the murder of Richard, but his words give the impression to subordinates that he wishes it. When the King learns of Richard's death, he repudiates the doer and deplores the

Julian Glover as Henry IV confronts Michael Maloney as Prince Hal, 1991.

Oscar Ashe as Henry Bolingbroke the warrior.

deed. *Richard II* ends with Henry pledging a pilgrimage to the Holy Land to atone for his part in his cousin's death.

In the two plays bearing his name, a marked lessening of physical and spiritual strength is noted in the character of Henry, and Shakespeare instead puts more emphasis on the King's son, Prince Hal, and his jolly drinking companion Sir John Falstaff. The main subject of *Henry IV Part 1* is the growth and maturing of Prince Hal. Falstaff functions as a surrogate father, and his world of irresponsibility is one which the Prince of Wales must ultimately reject, in favour of the world of duty represented by the King, his father. King Henry is faced with considerable unrest in the kingdom, but in due course Prince Hal comes to a better awareness of his duties and enters the conflict, where he distinguishes himself in his father's cause at the Battle of Shrewsbury. Rebellion continues in

Henry IV Part 2, as does the decline in the King's health, caused in part by his guilty conscience over Richard's murder. Shakespeare writes a brilliant death-bed scene for Henry IV, in which he is fully reconciled with his wayward son, and gives him sound advice for his future reign:

. . . Therefore, my Harry,
Be it thy course to busy giddy minds
With foreign quarrels, that action hence borne
    out
May waste the memory of the former days.
More would I, but my lungs are wasted so
That strength of speech is utterly denied me.
How I came by the crown, O God, forgive,
And grant it may with thee in true peace live!

After the theatres were re-opened at the time of the Restoration in 1660, the *Henry IV* plays became very popular, although in adapted form, and have continued to be popular ever since, but the star actors have tended to play Hal, Hotspur or Falstaff. In *Richard II*, it has been the frequent custom in recent years for two leading actors to alternate the roles of Richard and Bolingbroke. A recent example was a Royal Shakespeare Company production with Jeremy Irons and Michael Kitchen.

Bolingbroke, Roger
Historical character in *Henry VI Part 2* (*c*.1594). He is depicted as a sorcerer who converses with evil spirits.

Bona, Lady
Historical figure and character in *Henry VI Part 3* (*c*.1595). She is the sister-in-law of the French king and has been proposed as the bride of Edward IV, but he rejects her in favour of marriage with a commoner, Lady Elizabeth Woodville Grey.

Borachio
A follower of the villain, Don John, in *Much Ado About Nothing* (*c*.1599). He is a party to the machinations which result in the false denunciation of Hero at the altar, and thus part of the malevolent sub-plot in the comedy.

Bottom, Nick

A rustic in *A Midsummer Night's Dream* (1598) who is a weaver in Athens. He is the leader of a crew described as 'rude mechanicals', who are invited to perform a play for the Duke's wedding. Bottom is one of the very best of the author's clowns, mangling language and speaking in malapropisms, in the scenes where the play is rehearsed and ultimately staged, with disastrous results. On that level his character is entirely realistic. But he is also the subject of a trick by the fairy, Puck, who places an ass's head on Bottom and causes Titania, Queen of the Fairies, to fall in love with him in his transformed state. This episode, described as 'Bottom's Dream' is part of the fantasy side to the comedy. It provides Shakespeare with the classic 'beauty and the beast' motif which is the stuff of fairy tales. Bottom is the only mortal who actually meets any of the fairies, and in response to the question of which dream in the play is actually the dream referred to in the title, his is a strong contender, although not the only possibility.

ABOVE Nick Bottom in his ass's head with Titania and the Fairies.
BELOW James Cagney as Bottom in Max Reinhardt's 1935 Warner Bros. film.

Boult

A minor figure in *Pericles, Prince of Tyre* (*c.*1609). He is an employee in the brothel where the virtuous heroine, Marina, is imprisoned, and his task is to 'train and advertise' her. His name refers to the confining aspect of his function, but in fact he helps her to escape.

Bourbon, Jean, Duke of

Historical character, a French nobleman who features in *Henry V* (*c.*1599).

Bourbon, Lewis, Lord

A historical figure and minor character in *Henry VI Part 3* (*c.*1595), who is in the service of the King of France.

Bourchier, Cardinal Lord Thomas, Archbishop of Canterbury
(*c.*1404-86)

Historical figure and minor character in *Richard III* (*c.*1597).

Boy

A character known simply as 'boy' appears in *Henry VI Part 1* (*c.*1592); *The Merry Wives of Windsor* (*c.*1597); *Henry V* (*c.*1599); *Much Ado About Nothing* (*c.*1599); *Henry IV Part 2* (1600); *Troilus and Cressida* (*c.*1603); *Measure For Measure* (1604); *Antony and Cleopatra* (*c.*1608); *Henry VIII* (1613); and *The Two Noble Kinsmen* (*c.*1613). The role is minor in all cases except the boy who appears as Sir John Falstaff's page in *Henry V, Henry IV Part 2* and *Merry Wives*.

Boy

A small but telling presence in *Henry V* (*c.*1599). Having followed the late Sir John Falstaff as a page in *Henry IV Part 2* (1600), the boy is now a servant of Bardolph, Pistol and Nym, once companions of Falstaff. He accompanies these cronies to France as part of Henry's army, where he meets a grim death when the French raid the English camp and kill all the boys left to guard the baggage. In *The Merry Wives of Windsor* (*c.*1597), this same boy is known as Robin and is again Falstaff's page.

Boy, Edward Plantagenet, Earl of Warwick
(1475-99)

Historical but minor figure in *Richard III* (*c.*1597). He is the son of Clarence who, as elder brother of Richard, should have been further up the line of succession. Edward is imprisoned by his uncle, Richard, and we do not see him again, Richard has not felt it necessary to actually kill young Edward, because he is considered simple-minded, but his case is just one more circumstance which adds to the score of Richard's villainy.

Boyet

Follower of the Princess of France in *Love's Labour's Lost* (*c.*1598).

Brabantio

A secondary figure in *Othello* (1604), but nevertheless important as Desdemona's father. Her secret elopement with the Moor, Othello, is a radical action for an upper-class Venetian lady, and her father's outrage and distress is central to the plot. As Brabantio is a senator of Venice, he may command the ruling of the Duke on her action. The racial prejudice of Brabantio against his unwelcome son-in-law also sets Othello's subsequent doubt and jealousy in context.

Brakenbury, Sir Robert

Historical figure in *Richard III* (*c.*1597), Brakenbury is the commander of the Tower of London and thus the gaoler.

Brandon

Officer in *Henry VIII* (1613), who arrests Buckingham and Abergavenny. He may be the same character who appears later as the Duke of Suffolk.

Brandon, Sir William

Historical but minor character in *Richard III* (*c.*1597), a follower of Richmond, the future Henry VII.

Bretagne, Jean, Duke of

Historical but minor character in *Henry V* (*c.*1599), a follower of the French King.

Brook
Name used by Ford in *The Merry Wives of Windsor* (*c.*1597), when he is in disguise.

Brother
Minor character in *Henry VI Part 2* (*c.*1594), the sibling of Sir Humphrey Stafford, who accompanies his brother to put down the revolt led by Jack Cade.

Brother
Minor character in *The Two Noble Kinsmen* (*c.*1613), the brother of the gaoler.

Brutus, Junius
Possibly a historical figure, and a minor character in *Coriolanus* (1608). Brutus, a tribune of Rome, shares power with another tribune, Sicinius Velutus. They always appear together and there is no significant difference between them; they symbolise the power of the common people, as opposed to their enemy, the arrogant aristocrat Coriolanus. The crowd plays an important role in this play, and the tribunes' role in stirring them up is essential.

Brutus, Marcus
(*c.*85-42 BC)
Historical figure who is a major character in *Julius Caesar* (1599). Brutus is an extremely complex figure who seems, on the one hand, to be an honorable and patriotic man but, on the other, becomes the leader of the assassins of Caesar. This causes civil war in Rome, and ultimately Brutus's own destruction. Although Shakespeare telescopes two battles into one at the end of the play, he follows fairly accurately Plutarch's story of the defeat of Brutus at Philippi.

Caesar is Brutus's friend and mentor, but the increasing ambition of the former begins to alarm Rome's leading citizens. Brutus is persuaded to join the six conspirators and assassinate Caesar in the Forum. He is the last to stab, whereupon Caesar utters his famous dying words, 'Et tu, Brute? Then fall Caesar'. Brutus urges the conspirators to the ritual of bathing

Ben Kingsley as Brutus the conspirator, 1979.

their hands in Caesar's blood, but continues to delude himself that what he has done was for the best for his country. His fatal misjudgement in sparing Mark Antony and allowing him to speak at Caesar's funeral bears the seeds of Brutus's own downfall, for Antony, in the guise of a placatory funeral oration, succeeds in bringing the Roman populace to a full awareness of the horror of Caesar's death. As leader of the plot, Brutus insists on having his own way in all matters and gradually becomes as dictatorial as Caesar. Brutus has integrity, but his repeated wrong choices results in tragedy for the state and for himself. Antony's eulogy at the end on the death of Brutus is rightly celebrated as a gem of Shakespearean expression.

This was the noblest Roman of them all.
All the conspirators save only he
Did that they did in envy of great Caesar.
He only in a general honest thought
And common good to all made one of them.
His life was gentle, and the elements
So mixed in him that nature might stand up
And say to all the world 'This was a man!'

Buckingham, Edward Stafford, Duke of
Historical figure and minor character in *Henry VIII* (1613). Buckingham falls victim to the machinations of Cardinal Wolsey.

Buckingham, Henry Stafford, Duke of

Historical character and an important supporter of Gloucester in *Richard III* (*c*.1597). Once Gloucester has been crowned Richard III, he proves ungrateful. Buckingham deserts him and tries to join the invading Richmond's army but is executed by the King.

Buckingham, Sir Humphrey Stafford, Duke of

A real person who is depicted as an ally of the Duke of Suffolk against the Duke of Gloucester (later Richard III) in *Henry VI Part 2* (*c*.1594).

Bullcalf, Peter

One of the rustics in *Henry IV Part 2* (1600), who is recruited for the King's army by Sir John Falstaff but releases himself by a bribe from taking up duties.

Burgundy, Duke of

Minor character in *King Lear* (1608); Burgundy is a suitor for the King's youngest daughter, Cordelia, but rejects her on hearing that she now has no dowry.

Burgundy, Philip, Duke of (1396-1467)

Historical figure in *Henry VI Part 1* (*c*.1592) and *Henry V* (*c*.1599). He is an ally of the English, but changes his allegiance to France at the instigation of Joan la Pucelle (Joan of Arc) in *Henry VI*. As a younger man in *Henry V*, he functions as a peace-maker between the English and French Kings.

Bushy, Sir John

Historical figure in *Richard II* (*c*.1597) and a supporter of the King together with Bagot and Greene. Bushy and Greene are later executed by Bolingbroke.

Butts, Doctor William

A real person but minor figure in *Henry VIII* (1613). He was the personal physician of the King and the subject of a fine portrait by Hans Holbein the Younger.

C

Cade, Jack (d.1450)

The rebellion of Jack Cade takes up most of Act IV in *Henry VI Part 2* (*c*.1594). Cade, a historical Kentishman, is shown as incited to revolt by the Duke of York, but Shakespeare has taken very considerable liberties with the character of this commoner; he is also shown as a pretender to the throne. His villainies are preposterous, but his role is central to the author's theme of the importance of political stability.

Jack Cade, by C. Walter Hodges.

Cadwal

The name under which the King's son, Arviragus, is raised in *Cymbeline* (1611).

Caesar, Julius (102-44 BC)

Shakespeare's age regarded Julius Caesar as one of the world's greatest leaders, and thus his assassination was seen as a most foul crime. The title character in *Julius Caesar* (1599) is murdered in Act III,

John Woodvine's Julius Caesar, 1979.

Scene 1, in one of Shakespeare's most dramatic and effective stage moments. Although Caesar is not, therefore, a particularly large role, his character dominates the play, which is concerned not only with the death of Caesar and the reasons for it, but also the consequences. The continuing influence of Caesar is emphasised in the later scenes by his appearance in the form of a ghost to haunt his murderer, Brutus, on the eve of the fatal battle, saying '. . . thou shalt see me at Philippi.' And in the final scene of the play, Brutus speaks of the ghost as having appeared to him twice.

In the first half of the play, Julius Caesar seems older than his 52 years. He is depicted as both a strong and wise leader, and an imperious tyrant, who often refers to himself as 'we', or even in the third person. Clearly he is beginning to take himself too seriously for the good of the country, and the moral ambiguity surrounding his murder is the dilemma of the play. Shakespeare makes extensive use of his source, Plutarch's *Lives of the Noble Grecians and Romans*.

Caesar, Octavius
(63 BC-AD14)
Major historical figure, who took the title of Augustus as Emperor after the events in the two plays in which Shakespeare uses him as a character, *Julius Caesar* (1599) and *Antony and Cleopatra* (1608). The playwright is concerned with Octavius as a young man; in the former play he is described by Cassius as 'a peevish schoolboy', and in the latter by Cleopatra as 'the scarce-bearded Caesar'. In *Julius Caesar* his role as the nephew and adopted son of Julius Caesar is important, but he is only active near the end of the play when, having formed a triumvirate with Mark Antony and Lepidus, he opposes Cassius and Brutus, the assassins of Julius Caesar.

In *Antony and Cleopatra*, Octavius is a much more central character. His personality is contrasted strongly with the lovers, who are guided by emotion, whereas Octavius is shown as cold reason

personified. While ruthless, he is not heartless; he loves his sister, Octavia, and is fully able to appreciate the better qualities of the lovers, although he does not sympathise with their excesses. He is a born leader, and at the end represents political stability; in Act IV he says, 'The time of universal peace is near'. This *'pax Romana'* was seen in Shakespeare's day as the manifestation of the will of God, since the age of Augustus ushered in the Christian era. Thus Octavius Caesar seems to achieve a dignity at the conclusion which reaches beyond the world of the play.

Caius
A very minor and silent figure in *Titus Andronicus* (c.1594).

Caius
The name adopted by Kent in *King Lear* (1608) as part of his disguise as a commoner.

Caius, Doctor
A suitor to Anne Page in the sub-plot of *The Merry Wives of Windsor* (c.1597). As a Frenchman, he is a somewhat stereotyped figure, mangling his English.

Calchas
A legendary figure who appears in *Troilus and Cressida* (c.1603), he is a Trojan priest and the father of Cressida.

Caliban
One of Shakespeare's most imaginative fantasy figures, Caliban is found in *The Tempest* (1611). He is a sub-human character whose evil tendencies have to be kept in sharp check by his master, Prospero. The offspring of a witch and a devil, he is supernatural, but has no unusual powers. Prospero and his daughter, Miranda, have freed Caliban from imprisonment, taken him into their island home and taught him language. Although Caliban is somewhat simple-minded, he can show poetic powers of speech. For all his evil-doing, he recognises his folly at the end and

Michael Hordern as Caliban, 1952.

expresses his intent to 'seek grace'. His character is contrasted to the airy spirit, Ariel, who represents Good; Caliban is definitely earth-bound and represents baser animal instincts.

Calphurnia
A historical character and the wife of Caesar in *Julius Caesar* (1599). She is alarmed by bad omens, and pleads with her husband not to go to the Senate on 'the Ides of March', but he insists on doing so and, of course, goes to his death. Her role is small, and we see her only in the context of the devoted wife.

Cambio
The name Lucentio takes in *The Taming of the Shrew* (c.1594) when disguised, in order to further his wooing of Bianca.

Cambridge, Richard, Earl of
Historical character in *Henry V* (c.1599), a traitor who is executed for the attempted assassination of Henry V, before he leaves England for the campaign in France.

Camillo
An old servant of King Leontes in *The Winter's Tale* (1611). An important secondary character, he aids his King by disobeying him, and thus helps to effect the reconciliation of Leontes with his former friend, King Polixenes of Bohemia, whom Leontes wrongly suspected of adultery with his Queen.

Campeius, Cardinal Laurence
A historical character in *Henry VIII* (1613), Campeius is the Pope's ambassador to King Henry concerning the King's proposed divorce from Queen Katharine.

Canidius (Publius Canidius Crassus)
A very minor but historical figure in *Antony and Cleopatra* (1608), one of Antony's generals.

Caphis
A servant in *Timon of Athens* (c.1604).

Captain
A small part which is cast as a male of military age, and is found in *Henry VI Part 1* (c.1592); *Henry VI Part 2* (c.1594); *Titus Andronicus* (c.1594); *Richard II* (1597); *Twelfth Night* (1602); *Hamlet* (c.1602); *Macbeth* (1606); *King Lear* (1608); *Antony and Cleopatra* (1608); and *Cymbeline* (1611) where we find three.

Capuchius, Lord
Historical character in *Henry VIII* (1613), an ambassador from the Holy Roman Empire to England.

Capulet
The father of the heroine in *Romeo and Juliet* (1597) and an important secondary character. The Capulets have a deadly rivalry with another Veronese family, the Montagues, of whom Romeo is the heir. Capulet, a strict father, insists that his daughter marry to suit his wishes, a principal cause of the tragedy which claims the lives of the two lovers.

Bob Peck as Camillo, 1976.

Capulet
A minor character in *Romeo and Juliet* (1597), an aged relative in Juliet's family.

Capulet, Lady
The mother of Juliet in *Romeo and Juliet* (1597), and a rather unsympathetic parent. In the tomb scene where the fathers of the lovers are reconciled over the bodies of their dead children, Lady Capulet is present but does not speak.

Carlisle, Thomas Merke, Bishop of
Historical figure in *Richard II* (1597), who accompanies Richard on his return from Ireland to face Henry Bolingbroke. Carlisle is the only one to defend Richard at his deposition.

Carpenter
A walk-on in *Julius Caesar* (1599).

Carrier
Either of two walk-on characters in *Henry IV Part 1* (1598).

Casca, Publius Servius
One of the conspirators in *Julius Caesar* (1599), who speaks one of the author's most frequently quoted lines, 'It was Greek to me'. He is the first to stab Caesar, but after the assassination disappears from the play.

Ronald Pickup as Cassius watches John Gielgud's Caesar die, 1977.

Emma Hamilton as Cassandra, etching based on a painting by George Romney.

Cassandra
A Trojan princess in classical mythology and character in *Troilus and Cressida* (*c*.1603). She has the gift of prophecy, and twice predicts the fall of Troy.

Cassio
Secondary character in *Othello* (1604), also known as Michael Cassio. He is a Florentine officer serving under Othello, and incurs the hatred of the play's villain, Iago, because Cassio has been appointed lieutenant, a post coveted by Iago. The latter, pretending friendship, gets Cassio drunk and sets Roderigo on him, with the result that the lieutenant is discovered by Othello drunk and disorderly on duty and so is demoted. Even more insidiously, Iago wrongfully implicates Cassio with Othello's new wife, Desdemona, which causes the ultimate tragedy. Cassio is portrayed as a worthy young man, but rather too gullible.

Cassius (Caius Cassius Longinus) (d. 42 BC)
An actual person, one of the main conspirators in *Julius Caesar* (1599), and shown as cynical and ambitious. With Brutus, on whose sense of honour he plays, he leads the forces opposing Mark Anthony and Octavius Caesar after the assassination of Julius Caesar. Cassius is a good soldier, but he is hot-tempered. Julius Caesar's description early in the

play is foreboding:

Let me have men about me that are fat,
Sleek-headed men, and such as sleep a-nights.
Yon Cassius has a lean and hungry look.
He thinks too much. Such men are dangerous.

Cassius is a character frequently met with
in Elizabethan drama, the machiavel, the
cynical political villain whose actions are
based on the doctrines expounded by
Machiavelli in *The Prince* (1513).
Shakespeare follows his sources, Plutarch
and others, for the life of Cassius who,
like Brutus, dies at the battle of Philippi.

Catesby, Sir William
The historical Catesby was a lawyer, but
in *Richard III* (c.1597) he is a follower of
Richard's who lacks any particular
personality and is used as a messenger.
He is executed after the Battle of
Bosworth Field.

Cathness, Thorfin Sigurdsson, Earl of
Minor historical character in *Macbeth*
(1606), he is a Scottish nobleman who
joins the army led by Macduff and
Malcolm against Macbeth.

Cato
Minor character in *Julius Caesar* (1599).
A soldier in the army of Brutus, he claims
that he is the son of the famous Marcus
Cato, a historical character who was an
opponent of Julius Caesar. He is also
depicted as brother to Portia, Brutus's
wife, who was certainly the daughter of
the famous Cato.

Cawdor, Thane of
A title granted to the hero in *Macbeth*
(1606).

Celia
The secondary heroine in *As You Like It*
(1600), the cousin of the leading lady,
Rosalind. Celia's father Frederick has
usurped the dukedom from Rosalind's
father and banished the latter to the
Forest of Arden. When Duke Frederick
likewise banishes Rosalind, the two girls
run off together in disguise to the forest.

Celia's last-minute marriage at the end to
the minor villain, Oliver, is a weak
resolution to her otherwise lively and
enjoyable story.

Ceres
The classical goddess of harvests, who
appears in the brief masque scene in *The
Tempest* (1611).

Cerimon, Lord
A noble doctor in *Pericles, Prince of Tyre*
(c.1609), who revives the seemingly dead
Thaisa, wife of Pericles.

Cesario
The name taken by Viola when in male
disguise in *Twelfth Night* (1602).

Chamberlain
Minor character in *Henry IV Part 1*
(1598), who works in an inn.

Chamberlain
Minor character in *Henry VIII* (1613), an
attendant in the King's household.

Chancellor
Minor character in *Henry VIII* (1613), a
functionary in the King's government.

Charles VI, King of France
Minor historical figure in *Henry V*
(c.1599), who is the opponent of the
English King. Being elderly and
somewhat dim-witted, he is kept in the
background of the French court,
functioning as a figurehead.

Charles
A minor figure who appears only in the
early wrestling scene in *As You Like It*
(1600). Charles, the Duke's wrestler, is
unexpectedly defeated by the young hero,
Orlando.

Charmian
Secondary character in *Antony and
Cleopatra* (1608), possibly a real woman,
as she is given a brief mention in
Plutarch's *Lives*. Charmian is more than
just the conventional stage confidante of

the heroine. She is the more important of the Queen's two female attendants, and it is clear that she and Cleopatra love each other. Charmian is humorous, spirited, utterly loyal and brave to the end, where she follows her mistress's suicide with her own. It is she who makes the fatal suggestion that Cleopatra should let Antony think she has committed suicide, which leads to his premature death.

Chatillon (Chatillion)
Minor character in *King John* (*c.*1595), an ambassador from the King of France.

Chichele, Henry, Archbishop of Canterbury
A character in the early stages of *Henry V* who is called upon to outline the case for the king's claim to the French throne. As this is inevitably immensely complicated, the Archbishop is usually depicted as a doddering old man delivering a lengthy and rather comic speech, but the speech, as the basis for the King's invasion of France, is deadly serious.

Chief Justice, Lord
The highest-ranking judicial official in England, who appears as a character in *Henry IV Part 2* (1600). He chastises Sir John Falstaff on two occasions and has earlier imprisoned the Prince of Wales for a minor offence, but is nonetheless confirmed in his office by Henry V, and carries out his immensely symbolic decision to banish Falstaff.

Children
Minor figures in *The Merry Wives of Windsor* (*c.*1597), who take part in the tricking of Falstaff in Windsor Great Forest at the end of this farce.

Chiron
One of two sons of Tamora, Queen of the Goths, in *Titus Andronicus* (*c.*1594). These brothers commit the horrible rape and mutilation of Lavinia, Titus's daughter, and also murder Bassianus, the Emperor's brother, in this grotesque revenge tragedy.

Chorus
Although many characters act in a chorus-like fashion in Shakespeare's plays, only two are actually named 'Chorus'. The device of a chorus comes from ancient Greek drama, where it was performed by a group. Well before Shakespeare's time, a one-man chorus was in use in European drama, and he follows this pattern in *Henry V* (*c.*1599) and *Romeo and Juliet* (1597). In both cases, they are male figures, who have no personality of their own but are merely narrators.

In *Romeo and Juliet* Chorus speaks the opening passage, and also a passage which opens Act II. In each case, the speech is in the form of a sonnet (14 lines). The first one gives a full summary of the action of the play, leaving no element of suspense as to its outcome.

Chorus in *Henry V* (*c.*1599) has more extensive speeches, and the one which precedes Act I is especially famous for what it tells us about the conditions at the Globe Theatre (see Introduction). The Chorus likewise gives a long speech to introduce each of the other acts, and speaks the final lines of the play, which point forward to the reign of Henry VI. As the chorus in *Henry V* is so celebrated and has such lengthy and eloquent speeches, he is usually played by an experienced performer, such as David Garrick in the 1750s.

Ian McDiarmid as Chorus in *Henry V*, 1984.

Cicero, M. Tullius
Historical character in *Julius Caesar* (1599). His is not an important role, but he is a senator of Rome.

Cinna, Caius Helvetius
An historical but minor figure in *Julius Caesar* (1599). A poet, he is the victim of a mob of plebians, who mistake him for Cinna, one of the assassins of Caesar.

Cinna, Lucius Cornelius the Younger
Historical but minor character in *Julius Caesar* (1599), one of the conspirators who stab Caesar.

Citizen
One citizen or a group of citizens is found in *Henry VI Part 2* (*c.*1594); *King John* (*c.*1595); *Richard III* (*c.*1597); *Romeo and Juliet* (1597); and *Coriolanus* (1608). In the last they are particularly important to the theme of power politics. In productions of the last hundred years or so, female as well as male extras have been used, and also people of different ages.

Clarence, George, Duke of (1449-78)
Historical figure in *Henry VI Part 3* (*c.*1595) and *Richard III* (*c.*1597), the brother of Richard. Clarence is ahead of Richard in the line of succession, and thus must be dispensed with in the villainous hero's climb to the throne, Clarence's death scene in the Tower of London is written in some of the most beautiful lyric poetry in the play.

Clarence, Thomas, Duke of
An actual but minor figure in *Henry IV Part 2* (1600) and in *Henry V* (*c.*1599). He is the son of the first King and the younger brother of the second.

Claudio
An important secondary character in *Much Ado About Nothing* (*c.*1599); Claudio and Hero are one of the two sets of lovers with whom this romantic comedy is concerned. A rather shallow young nobleman, who has seen military duty in the entourage of Don Pedro, he loves Hero on first sight, but rejects her at the altar on flimsy evidence of her unfaithfulness.

Claudio
An important secondary character in *Measure For Measure* (1604) whose sister, the play's heroine, has entered a convent. Claudio, finding himself imprisoned and condemned to death for getting his betrothed, Juliet, pregnant, appeals to his sister, Isabella, for help. When Isabella in turn pleads with Angelo, the ruling authority in the Duke's absence, Angelo requires her to choose between her virginity and Claudio's life. In a moving scene in the prison, Claudio tries to be noble, but ends up asking his sister to submit in order to save him.

Johnston Forbes-Robertson as Claudio.

Claudius
Minor character in *Julius Caesar* (1599), a soldier in the army of Brutus.

Claudius, King
This major figure in *Hamlet* (*c.*1602) is King of Denmark as the play opens, having succeeded his brother, King Hamlet. Claudius is the uncle of Prince Hamlet, and has married Queen Gertrude, widow of the late King, very hastily. At the beginning of the play, it is revealed to Prince Hamlet by the ghost of his late father that Claudius murdered him. Claudius comes to a better awareness of his gross sin, and he seems to truly love Gertrude. Nevertheless, he sinks further into evil and attempts to have Prince Hamlet murdered. Claudius's initial crime in killing his brother and usurping his throne is presented not only as a private, family sin, but as one which totally permeates the body politic. Moreover his marriage with his sister-in-law is seen in the context of the play.

Andrew Cruikshank as King Claudius.

incestuous. Although a villain, Claudius is a fully human character, developed in great detail by the dramatist; he is a generally competent monarch when conducting business. Claudius inadvertently kills Gertrude by means of a poisoned cup, and finally meets his death at the hands of Prince Hamlet.

Cleomenes and Dion
These minor characters in *The Winter's Tale* (1611) act virtually as one, having no distinct characteristics. Followers of King Leontes, they are sent by him to consult the oracle.

Cleon
A small part in *Pericles, Prince of Tyre* (*c*.1609), the governor of Tharsus and husband of Dionyza. Marina, daughter of Pericles, is left in their care.

Cleopatra, Queen of Egypt (68-30 BC)
Historical figure and title character in *Antony and Cleopatra* (1608), one of the author's very greatest creations. She is an experienced courtesan, having been the mistress both of Julius Caesar and of Pompey before the play opens. Her means of holding the attention of Mark

Antony are cunning in the extreme. The famous description of her spoken by Antony's friend, Enobarbus, is taken very closely from Plutarch's account, except that Shakespeare has cast it into incomparable verse.

Age cannot wither her, nor custom stale
Her infinite variety. Other women cloy
The appetites they feed, but she makes
    hungry
Where most she satisfies. For vilest things
Become themselves in her, that the holy
    priests
Bless her when she is riggish.

There is considerable comedy in the character of Cleopatra who is, much of the time, an actress; her theatrical nature is also put to magnificent use by the author in the nature and trappings of her suicide in Act V. Cleopatra genuinely loves Antony, but this passion seems to grow as the play progresses and reaches its height after his own suicide. Of her actual physical appearance, we are given only clues. Plutarch says she was 38, and Antony considerably older. She refers to herself as 'wrinkled deep in time', and mentions her 'salad days, when I was green in judgment, cold in blood'. Other characters refer to her as having a 'tawny front', as 'gipsy', 'great fairy', 'charm', 'Eastern star', and as the personification, 'Egypt'. Octavius, looking at her dead body, sees still 'her strong toil of grace'.

We see something of her role as Queen in dealing with ambassadors and messengers, and she does go to the Battle of Actium with Antony, insisting against advice that she, 'as president of my kingdom, will appear there for a man'. Yet the greatest interest of the character, and indeed the supreme challenge for the actress, is to transcend her earlier portrayal as the teasing courtesan, to the point where she is transformed into a noble and tragic figure. The text effects this through her noble response to the death of Antony. Her decision to kill herself is not only to escape the humiliation which she knows Octavius intends for her in Rome, but principally because she sees it as the only way to be worthy of Antony. Hers is a triumphant, and highly dramatic, affirmation of life and love. In Act V, locked in her monument to avoid Caesar, she prepares her final act.

Give me my robe. Put on my crown. I have
immortal longings in me. Now no more
The juice of Egypt's grape shall moist this lip.
Yare, yare, good Iras, quick – methinks I hear
Antony call. I see him rouse himself
To praise my noble act. I hear him mock
The luck of Caesar, which the gods give men
To excuse their after wrath. Husband, I come.
Now to that name my courage prove my title!
I am fire and air; my other elements
I give to baser life.

The stage history of the play is partly discussed under the entry for 'Antony'. It is astonishing, and disappointing, to learn that the greatest actress of all times, Sarah Siddons, never took the role. In the nineteenth century, Lillie Langtry had moderate success with her performance of the character. In modern times the role has been played by Dame Edith Evans, Dame Peggy Ashcroft, Vivien Leigh, Vanessa Redgrave, Dame Diana Rigg, Dame Judi Dench, and in America most notably by the incomparable Katherine Cornell.

Clerk
Minor character in *Henry VI Part 2* (*c.*1594), called Emmanuel, who is executed by Jack Cade's rebels.

Clifford, Lord John
A character in Parts 2 and 3 of *Henry VI* (*c.*1594/*c.*1595), who avenges the death of his father, Thomas Clifford, by killing the Duke of York and his son, Rutland. The younger Clifford is particularly savage.

Clifford, Lord Thomas
The father of the above, he is a character in *Henry VI Part 2* (*c.*1594), and backs King Henry's cause against the Yorkists.

Clitus
Minor historical figure in *Julius Caesar* (1599), a soldier in the army of Brutus.

Cloten
The uncouth son of the Queen in *Cymbeline* (1611), Cloten is rejected as a suitor by the heroine, Imogen. He then plans to rape her and kill her husband, but for the most part is shown as a comic villain. Shakespeare kills him off when he is no longer needed.

Lillie Langtry plays a sultry Cleopatra, 1890.

Clown
There are a number of clowns in the plays of Shakespeare: they are male rustics probably acted originally by Robert Armin (d.1615) and Will Kempe (d.*c.*1608), the author's colleagues. An example of an early clown is found in *Titus Andronicus* (*c.*1594), entering with two pigeons in a basket.

Clown
Either of two characters in *Hamlet* (*c.*1602), who function as grave diggers in Act V, preparing the grave of Ophelia. Their conversation with Hamlet covers philosophical and political issues, but mainly serves as comic relief before the approaching tragic climax.

Clown
A jester in *Othello* (1604), who is in the retinue of the hero.

Clown
A pretended fig-seller in *Antony and Cleopatra* (1608) whom the Queen is able to smuggle into her prison, the monument. He brings in his basket the asps with which she intends to kill herself. Although she does not take them from the basket in his presence, whatever the Director is intending to use must be in his basket, and thus he is a part of a very tricky piece of stage business. As a typical country bumpkin, his role is again that of comic relief to heighten the tragic climax.

Clown
A minor figure in *The Winter's Tale* (1611), whose father has discovered the baby which will grow into Perdita. Together they take the infant home, and the clown becomes her foster-brother.

Cobbler
A commoner who is a very minor character in *Julius Caesar* (1599).

Cobweb
One of Shakespeare's marvellously fanciful names for a fairy in *A Midsummer Night's Dream* (1598). Whether male or female is not too important, but Cobweb should be tiny, and thus children, or even puppets, have been used in productions.

Colchester, William, Abbot of Westminster
Historical figure in *Richard II* (1597), a conspirator against Henry Bolingbroke. After the deposition of King Richard, the Abbot, together with the Duke of Aumerle and the Bishop of Carlisle, plot to kill Henry, the usurper, but their plot is discovered. Although the historical Abbot was pardoned by Bolingbroke after he became Henry IV, in the play he seems to have died of a guilty conscience.

Colevile (Coleville) of the Dale, Sir John
Minor historical figure in *Henry IV Part 2* (1600), a rebel knight captured by Falstaff.

Cominius
Legendary character in *Coriolanus* (*c.*1608), a friend of the hero and commander of the Roman troops.

Commoner
Any of several walk-ons in *Julius Caesar* (1599), *Coriolanus* (*c.*1608) and *Henry VIII* (1613).

Commons
A group of walk-ons in *Henry VI Part 2* (*c.*1594), members of the Parliament assembled at Bury St Edmunds.

Conrad
Follower of the villain, Don John, in *Much Ado About Nothing* (*c.*1599).

Conspirators
Minor figures in *Coriolanus* (*c.*1608) who are followers of his rival, Aufidius.

Constable of France, Charles D'Albert (Delabreth)
Minor historical figure in *Henry V* (*c.*1599), a high-ranking French officer who dies in the Battle of Agincourt.

Cordelia's Portion (detail) by Ford Madox Brown.

Constance, Duchess of Brittany

Historical figure who is an important character in *King John* (*c*.1595). Constance is the mother of the young Prince Arthur, claimant to the English throne. Her character is portrayed as highly emotional.

Cordelia

The youngest daughter of *King Lear* (1608). Knowing that she is soon to marry, Cordelia refuses to declare that all her love is for her father when, in his senility, he requires his three daughters to make declarations of their love in front of the whole court. He divides his kingdom according to their answers, and Cordelia's answer results in her banishment. The King of France takes her to wife without a dowry, and she disappears from the play for a very considerable time. After much suffering, the aged King is reunited with his favourite daughter just before their joint deaths. She is shown as so angelic, however, as to have very little variation in her character.

Corin

A rustic in *As You Like It* (1600), Corin is an elderly shepherd in the Forest of Arden.

Coriolanus, Martius

A legendary character in Plutarch's *Lives*, not now thought to be historical, whom the playwright has taken as his title figure in *Coriolanus* (*c*.1608). He is a famous Roman soldier whose excessive arrogance leads to his downfall and death. He has had a stern upbringing from his formidable mother, Volumnia, which has nevertheless left him emotionally immature. He refuses to compromise in the ruling of Rome, with the result that he is driven out of the city and joins Rome's enemies, the Volscians. Finally his mother persuades him to spare Rome, but this leads to Coriolanus's death at the hands of his rival, Aufidius. His relationship with his mother is perhaps the most complex part of his character; he loses his life rather than lose her approbation. His overbearing pride makes him an ideal tragic hero in some ways, but it is very hard for the audience to emphathise with him, and he achieves little self-awareness.

Richard Burbage was probably the original Coriolanus, but it has never been a consistently popular part, and was a failure with Garrick. Between 1789 and 1817, John Philip Kemble and his sister, Mrs Siddons, enacted an adaptation by Richard Brinsley Sheridan, the manager of the Drury Lane Theatre and virtuoso comic playwright. Kemble may be considered the definitive pre-twentieth-century interpreter; he made his farewell

Kenneth Branagh as Coriolanus, 1992.

John Philip Kemble as Coriolanus, after the painting by Sir Thomas Lawrence.

to the stage in the role in 1817, and was painted by Lawrence. Edwin Forrest was notably successful in the role in New York in the nineteenth century, and Laurence Olivier and Sybil Thorndike firmly established the play in the modern repertoire with Lewis Casson's 1938 staging. In 1959 Olivier repeated the part opposite Edith Evans, while in 1991, Sir Ian McKellen was outstanding in a Royal National Theatre production.

Cornelius
Minor character in *Hamlet* (*c.*1602), who is sent as an ambassador to Norway from the King of Denmark.

Cornelius
Minor character in *Cymbeline* (1611), a doctor who provides the wicked Queen with a poison.

Cornwall, Duke of
An important secondary character in *King Lear* (1608), Cornwall is the evil husband of the equally evil Regan, one of Lear's two older daughters. Cornwall's worst act is to put out Gloucester's eyes with the spurs of his boots; for this outrage, he is killed by an angry servant.

Costard
A clown in *Love's Labour's Lost* (*c.*1598) who figures in the sub-plot, in which he mixes up love letters. He is a character type derived from the commedia dell'arte tradition, and even traceable back to Roman comedy.

Countrymen
Group of minor figures in *The Two Noble Kinsmen* (*c.*1613).

Court, Alexander
Minor character in *Henry V* (*c.*1599), who meets the King incognito on the eve of the Battle of Agincourt.

Courtesan
Minor character in *The Comedy of Errors* (*c.*1594).

Crab
Minor but delightful character in *The Two Gentlemen of Verona* (*c.*1598), the pet dog of the comic servant, Launce, with whom he has two hilarious scenes. Unlike the bear in *The Winter's Tale* (1611), there is no question but that Crab is a real, live, on-stage animal, the only one in Shakespeare's plays. Although the name refers to crab apple and suggests that the dog should be small and sour in expression, a large Irish wolfhound was used with great success in a recent production by the Royal Shakespeare Company.

Cranmer, Thomas, Archbishop of Canterbury
A historical figure in *Henry VIII* (1613) and an important advocate of the Protestant succession. He baptises the infant Princess Elizabeth at the end of the play and predicts glory for her reign.

Cressida
Legendary Trojan princess and title character in *Troilus and Cressida* (*c.*1603). She is the lover of Troilus, but she betrays him in favour of the Greek, Diomedes.

Crier
Minor court functionary at the trial of Queen Katharine in *Henry VIII* (1613).

Cromwell, Thomas
(c.1485-1540)
Historical figure in *Henry VIII* (1613), he is a secretary to Cardinal Wolsey. When the Cardinal's fall from favour is imminent, Cromwell remains loyal to him. His rise to become an ally of the King is seen in the later scenes.

Cupid
A lady in a masque in *Timon of Athens* (c.1604).

Curan
Minor character in *King Lear* (1608), a follower of Gloucester.

Curio
Minor character in *Twelfth Night* (1602), a follower of Count Orsino.

Curtis
Minor character in *The Taming of the Shrew* (c.1594), servant of Petruchio.

Cymbeline
(d.c. AD 40)
Title character of *Cymbeline* (1611), taken by Shakespeare from Holinshed's *Chronicles*. The historical character is generally called Cunobelinus and was ruler of the Celtic tribes in south-east England. In the play he is the aged King

Amanda Root as Cressida, 1991.

of Britain and father of the heroine, Imogen, and his role is secondary. Influenced by his wicked Queen, stepmother to Imogen, who wants Imogen to marry her own son Cloten, he banishes Imogen's husband Posthumus. His character is passive and not fully developed.

D

Dardanius
Minor historical character in *Julius Caesar* (1599).

Daughter
Minor nameless character in *Pericles, Prince of Tyre* (c.1609), who is the incestuous lover of her father, King Antiochus of Syria.

Daughter
The deranged daughter of the gaoler, who falls in love with one of the title characters in *The Two Noble Kinsmen* (c.1613).

Dauphin Charles, The
(1403-61)
Historical character found in *Henry VI Part 1* (c.1592). He subsequently became Charles VII of France, but in the play is called by the title accorded the French heir to the throne, Dauphin.

Dauphin Lewis, The
(1187-1226)
Historical character found in *King John* (c.1595), who became Louis VIII of France.

Dauphin Lewis, The
A secondary character in *Henry V* (c.1599), known by that name and spelling in the First Folio of 1623, but simply as Dauphin in the Quarto of 1600. He is the heir to the French King who opposes King Henry, and is an arrogant man who insultingly sends tennis balls to Henry and who, in the absence of his elderly father, leads the French at Agincourt.

Davy
A minor character in *Henry IV Part 2* (1600), steward to Justice Shallow.

Decius (Decimus) Brutus
Historical figure who is one of the assassins in *Julius Caesar* (1599), and is of secondary importance.

Decretas
Various spellings are found for this historical character, who is an attendant of the hero in *Antony and Cleopatra* (1608).

Deiphobus
Legendary character, a Trojan soldier in *Troilus and Cressida* (c.1603).

Demetrius
A son of Queen Tamora in *Titus Andronicus* (c.1594), who is thoroughly villainous.

Demetrius
An important character in *A Midsummer Night's Dream* (1598). He and Hermia are one of two pairs of lovers who get lost in the forest and are subject to the mix-ups of Puck, the fairy.

Demetrius
Follower of Antony in *Antony and Cleopatra* (1608).

Dennis
A servant of Orlando's wicked brother, Oliver, in *As You Like It* (1600).

Denny, Sir Anthony
Minor historical character in *Henry VIII* (1613), a member of the King's court.

Desdemona
An aristocratic Venetian girl in *Othello* (1604). She is the leading female character and is exceedingly interesting from a modern point of view, on account of her radical decision to marry a black, the Moorish soldier Othello. This courageous and loving act bears the seeds of her destruction, however, as the insecurity

Desdemona chided by her husband, by C. Walter Hodges.

which her new husband feels in her love leads him into rash suspicion of her virtue, and makes him the easy dupe of the villain, Iago. Ultimately Othello kills the new bride whom he so loves. Desdemona is a girl of unusual intelligence and imagination, and indeed one of the author's most compelling studies of young womanhood.

Diana
A secondary character in *All's Well That Ends Well* (c.1603), whose character is slight, sufficient only for her role as 'the other woman' in the bed trick played by the heroine, Helena, on Bertram, whom she loves. Diana is a virginal maiden who is pursued by Bertram and agrees to help Helena by letting Helena take her place. This bed trick appears also in *Measure For Measure* (1604), where it is equally repugnant and unconvincing.

Diana
A Roman goddess found as a character in *Pericles, Prince of Tyre* (c.1609), where she appears to the hero in a vision.

Dick the Butcher
Minor character in *Henry VI Part 2* (c.1594), a follower of the rebel, Jack Cade.

Diomedes
Legendary character who features in *Troilus and Cressida* (c.1603). He plays a

minor role in the Trojan War, but when his duties include supervising an exchange of prisoners, he encounters Cressida, whom he seduces. His amorality contributes to the cynical atmosphere in this very long play.

Diomedes
Minor historical character in *Antony and Cleopatra* (1608), a servant of the Queen of Egypt.

Dionyza
A secondary female character in *Pericles, Prince of Tyre* (*c.*1609). The hero leaves his infant daughter, Marina, in the care of Dionyza and her husband, Cleon, not realising that Dionyza's jealousy will lead her to attempt Marina's life.

Doctor
A minor character in *King Lear* (1608), who attends the aged monarch in the final scenes of the tragedy and counsels the King's grieving daughter, Cordelia.

Doctor
A minor character in *Macbeth* (1606), who attends Lady Macbeth towards the end of the tragedy, as she begins to lose her reason and slip towards suicide. He is present with a female attendant during Lady Macbeth's famous 'sleepwalking scene'.

Doctor
A minor character in *Macbeth* (1606), but different from the above. He is an Englishmen serving King Edward the Confessor (who does not appear in the play), and who advises Malcolm and Macduff.

Doctor
A minor character in *The Two Noble Kinsmen* (*c.*1613) who ministers to the disturbed daughter of the gaoler.

Doctor of Divinity
Otherwise referred to as 'Priest', this figure officiates at the funeral of Ophelia in *Hamlet* (*c.*1602).

George Rose plays Dogberry to John Moffat's Verges, 1952.

Dogberry
One of Shakespeare's very best rustics, Dogberry is the constable in charge of the watch in *Much Ado About Nothing* (*c.*1599). More than any other character in Shakespeare, Dogberry mangles language and speaks in malapropisms, such as 'Comparisons are odorous'. Inept though he and his cohorts are, they do apprehend (comprehend, according to Dogberry) the villains. Dogberry is very funny, but it takes a talented actor to effect the malapropisms clearly enough for a modern audience.

Dolabella, Cornelius
Minor historical character in *Antony and Cleopatra* (1608) who is in the train of Octavius Caesar.

Don John
Character in *Much Ado About Nothing* (*c.*1599) whose villainy sets in motion the near-tragic sub-plot of the play. He is the brother of Don Pedro.

Don Pedro
A secondary character in *Much Ado About Nothing* (*c.*1599), who is the Prince of Arragon. He helps to further the romances of his subordinates, Claudio and Benedict, with Hero and Beatrice, respectively the daughter and niece of the Governor of Messina, whose court these three soldiers are visiting.

Donalbain
Historical figure in *Macbeth* (1606), Donalbain is the younger son of the murdered King Duncan. His role, however, is quite minor.

Dorcas
A sprightly shepherdess in the pastoral second half of *The Winter's Tale* (1611). Lightly sketched in, her minor character adds country atmosphere.

Doricles
The name taken by Prince Florizel when he disguises himself in *The Winter's Tale* (1611) in order to court the supposed shepherdess, Perdita.

Dorset, Thomas Grey, Marquis of
Minor historical character in *Richard III* (*c.*1597). Dorset is the son of Edward IV's widow, Queen Elizabeth Woodville Grey, by a previous marriage.

Douglas, Archibald, Earl of
Historical figure, noted for his military courage, who appears in *Henry IV Part 1* (1598) as the leader of the Scottish forces against Henry Bolingbroke.

Drawer
Any of several walk-on characters in *Henry IV Part 2* (1600), who are servants at the Boar's Head Tavern. Their task is to draw wine and serve it.

Dromio of Ephesus and Dromio of Syracuse
A pair of identical twins in *The Comedy of Errors* (*c.*1594), whose masters are also twins. Each pair were separated from their brother in a shipwreck in infancy and now, in adulthood, come into contact again, with complicated and hilarious results. The servants are of the stock type found in Roman drama.

Duke Senior
The more interesting of the two fathers in *As You Like It* (1600), he has lost his kingdom and been banished to the Forest of Arden by his brother, Duke Frederick. In the forest, the nameless Duke Senior is re-united with his daughter, Rosalind. Duke Senior's character is only sketchy but his rustic life in the woods with his followers is appealing, although it clearly has hardships.

Dull, Anthony
Minor character in *Love's Labour's Lost* (*c.*1598), another of the author's comic rustics who are given a symbolic name to indicate their function or chief character trait. Dull is a stupid constable.

Dumaine (Dumain)
One of the gentlemen in *Love's Labour's Lost* (*c.*1598) who, despite their good intentions, are unsuccessful in their attempt to follow the King's order and give up revels and love for a period and devote themselves to scholarship. Dumaine falls in love with Katharine, lady-in-waiting to the Prince of France. As with many roles in this play, his is a rather flat character.

Dumaine
Two identical small parts in *All's Well That Ends Well* (*c.*1603), they are lords who are brothers.

Duncan, King of Scotland (*c.*1001-39)
Historical person and an important character in *Macbeth* (1606). Duncan gives the impression of being very elderly, although clearly the real man was not. He is a good king and even his

Michael Williams as Dromio of Syracuse, 1976.

murderer, Macbeth, reflects on his exemplary qualities. Shakespeare portrays him as a trusting old man, which makes his murder the more horrendous. In an unusually short play, Duncan quits the stage quite early, although his influence continues until the end; his two sons figure in the resolution to the tragedy.

Dunois, Jean
See Bastard of Orleans.

Dutchman and Spaniard
Minor, non-speaking roles in *Cymbeline* (1611).

Edgar as Tom O'Bedlam with the mad Lear, by C. Walter Hodges.

E

Edgar
This young man is one of two brothers in *King Lear* (1608), both major characters, who are strongly contrasted. Edgar is the legitimate and virtuous son of the Duke of Gloucester, but through the machinations of his half-brother Edmund, Edgar is banished. The play is unusual among the tragedies in having a subplot, and the banishment of Edgar by his father reinforces the banishment of Cordelia by Lear in the main plot. Edgar goes into disguise as a roving madman, Tom O'Bedlam, and in that shape meets both Lear and Gloucester, whose now fallen and miserable state Edgar attempts to alleviate. At the end he forgives his wicked brother, whom he has mortally wounded in battle, and is one of the few survivors in this bleak masterwork.

Edmund
This young man is the second of two brothers who are central to *King Lear* (1608). Edmund, interestingly enough, has been given the name of Shakespeare's brother, who was an actor and is buried in London's Southwark Cathedral, near the Globe Theatre. In the play, Edmund is a machiavel, and his villainy is strongly energetic. He is the illegitimate son of the Duke of Gloucester, and plays off against each other Lear's two wicked daughters, both of whom are in love with him. Having conspired against his brother Edgar, he is nevertheless reconciled to him at the end. Edmund is responsible for the death sentence on Lear and his younger daughter, Cordelia. As he lies dying, Edmund attempts to rescind this, but it is too late to save Cordelia. Lear dies of old age and a broken heart, but not specifically by the action of Edmund.

Edward, Prince of Wales, later Edward V (1470-c.1483)
The elder of the so-called 'little princes in the Tower', a pivotal character in *Richard III* (c.1597). He is aged about thirteen and although he is never referred to as Edward V, his accession was of course automatic on the death of his father Edward IV. Plans for his coronation are

Isa Bowman and Bessie Hatton as the two princes in *Richard III*.

referred to, but never carried out as he and his younger brother are soon murdered by agents of their uncle, Richard. The demeanour of young Edward, his love for his younger brother, and his quick intelligence, make him an appealing figure in his brief stage time.

Edward Prince of Wales (1453-1471)

Edward is the heir of King Henry and Queen Margaret in *Henry VI Part 3* (*c*.1595), and is taken prisoner by the Yorkist faction at Tewkesbury and killed. Prince Edward's appearance is brief but chivalrous. Although not within the context of the play, he is married to Lady Anne Neville, later Queen to Richard III.

Edward IV, King of England (1442-83)

We meet this historical character in *Henry VI Parts 2 and 3* (*c*.1594/*c*.1595) and *Richard III* (*c*.1597). He is known as Edward, Earl of March, until the latter part of the trilogy, when he achieves the crown after the Yorkist faction is successful against the Lancasters. The Wars of the Roses continue, however, and he does not particularly distinguish himself as king. His lust for the Lady Elizabeth Grey, a widow, is impolitic and leads to his renunciation of the French princess to whom he was committed. He marries Elizabeth, who brings more difficulties to his troubled reign. In the *Henry VI* trilogy we see Edward as a soldier and active politician. In *Richard III* (*c*.1597) he is depicted as an old man at death's door, yet his licentiousness, now with regard to Lady Jane Shore, is still stressed. His death is hastened by news of his brother Clarence's death, ordered by the future Richard III, allegedly on Edward's behalf. His appearance in this play is limited to one scene in Act II; his reign is not accurately treated by Shakespeare.

Egeon

An old man who is the father of the twins Antipholus in *The Comedy of Errors*

(*c*.1594), and the husband of Emilia, who is now an Abbess. Egeon has been separated from his long-lost family by a shipwreck, and his character functions only in the first and last scenes of the farce in order to frame the main action.

Egeus

A minor character in *A Midsummer Night's Dream* (1598), the father of one of the young heroines, Hermia. He is severe to her, insisting that she marry against her will.

Eglamour

Minor character in *The Two Gentlemen of Verona* (*c*.1598), a gentleman who is the confidant of Silvia, the heroine.

Egyptian

A messenger of the Queen of Egypt in *Antony and Cleopatra* (1608).

Elbow

Minor comic constable in *Measure For Measure* (1604).

Eleanor of Aquitaine, Queen of England (1122-1204)

One of the most important female figures in the Middle Ages, and a secondary character in *King John* (*c*.1595), of whom she is the mother. A strong woman and wise diplomat, she was a French heiress of huge territory and is the widow of Henry II. Her death just as John faces French invasion is devastating to him.

Frances Tomelty as Queen Elizabeth, with Antony Sher as Richard III, 1984.

Elizabeth I, Queen of England (1533-1603)

The baptism of the infant Elizabeth is the closing scene of *Henry VIII* (1613).

Elizabeth Woodville Grey, later Queen of England (1437-1492)

We meet this historical figure as Lady Elizabeth Grey in *Henry VI Part 3* (c.1595), in the small role of a supplicant to Edward IV for the restitution of her late husband's estates. She refuses to become his mistress, so Edward marries her. In *Richard III* (c.1597) she is a major character, as Queen Elizabeth, even though the King dies quite early in this play. She becomes an important adversary of her brother-in-law, Richard, and she is the mother of the so-called 'little princes in the Tower', whom Richard is alleged to have had murdered as they stood in his way to the throne. She is part of the chorus of three royal women, together with Queen Margaret and the old Duchess of Gloucester, in the symbolic scene outside the Tower where the women bemoan their fate. Later Queen Elizabeth must defend her daughter, Princess Elizabeth (who does not appear in the play), against the machinations of Richard, who wants to marry his niece. Queen Elizabeth is shown at all times as an admirable figure.

Ely, Bishop of

Silent figure at the trial of Queen Katharine in Henry VIII (1613).

Emilia

An important character in *Othello* (1604), Emilia is the wife of the villain, Iago, by whom she is genuinely duped, and she unknowingly aids his machinations by giving him Desdemona's handkerchief. She is also the confidante and true friend of the hapless heroine, Desdemona. She fearlessly opposes Othello's rash jealousy of his wife and, once aware of Iago's villainy, she denounces him boldly, for which he stabs her. The role has been outstandingly performed recently by Zoe Wanamaker in a Royal Shakespeare Company production which was filmed by the BBC.

Emilia

A very minor character in *The Winter's Tale* (1611), a lady-in-waiting to the heroine, Queen Hermione.

Emilia

A leading lady in *The Two Noble Kinsmen* (c.1613), both of whom love her. This causes the rupture in their friendship.

Emilia

See Abbess, the.

Enobarbus (Cnaeus Domitius Ahenobarbus)

Historical figure and important secondary character in *Antony and Cleopatra* (1608). Enobarbus is a battle-seasoned soldier, somewhat cynical but good-hearted. He is Antony's chief adviser and close friend, but becomes disenchanted with his General's dissolute ways. It is Enobarbus who describes the first meeting of the lovers, and who speaks the famous purple passage describing the Queen, beginning 'Age cannot wither her . . .' (see Cleopatra). When Antony learns that Enobarbus has deserted to Caesar, his response is charitable. This breaks Enobarbus's heart and he subsequently commits suicide.

Epilogue

The final speech of a play which, like the Chorus, is spoken by one person addressing the audience directly, and is usually a summation of some kind. Epilogues are found in *A Midsummer Night's Dream* (1598), spoken by Robin Goodfellow, also known as Puck; *Henry V* (*c*.1599), spoken by the Chorus; *Henry IV Part 2* (1600); *As You Like It* (1600), where Shakespeare calls attention to his very unusual device of having the epilogue spoken by a lady, Rosalind; *Twelfth Night* (1602), where the epilogue is actually a song by Feste; *Pericles, Prince of Tyre* (*c*.1609), spoken by John Gower, the Presenter; *The Tempest* (1611), spoken by Prospero; *Henry VIII* (1613), and *The Two Noble Kinsmen* (*c*.1613). Epilogues may be spoken by an impersonal male figure who is not a character in the play, or by a character from the play, usually male.

Eros

One of Antony's attendants in *Antony and Cleopatra* (1608). He is devoted to his master and rather than hold the sword for Antony to rush upon, in the manner of Roman suicides, kills himself.

Erpingham, Sir Thomas

Historical but minor figure in *Henry V* (*c*.1599), an officer in the King's army.

Escalus

A minor character, a subordinate of the Duke of Vienna in *Measure For Measure* (1604). Escalus is elderly and respected.

Escalus, Prince of Verona

The ruling authority in *Romeo and Juliet* (1597), but a small part. He is a stern man of mature years.

Escanes

A minor lord in *Pericles, Prince of Tyre* (*c*.1609).

Essex, Geoffrey Fitzpeter

Minor historical figure in *King John* (*c*.1595), a walk-on follower of the King.

Brian Blessed as Exeter in *Henry V*, 1984.

Evans, Sir Hugh

A delightful but secondary character in *The Merry Wives of Windsor* (*c*.1597), Sir Hugh Evans is a Welshman who serves the dual function in Windsor of clergyman and schoolmaster. He has a talent for putting his foot in it, and it has been speculated that the character is a portrait of Shakespeare's own schoolmaster at Stratford. Sir Hugh conducts the famous 'Latin scene' in which Master William Page is put through his Latin grammar, without notable success, from the standard text which the author would have known as a schoolboy himself, Lily's *Grammar*. The teacher at the time when Shakespeare is presumed to have been at the King Edward VI Grammar School was a Welshman, one Thomas Jenkins.

Executioner

Minor character in *The Comedy of Errors* (*c*.1594), *King John* (*c*.1595), and *The Two Noble Kinsmen* (*c*.1613).

Exeter, Henry Holland, Duke of

Historical but minor figure in *Henry VI Part 3* (*c*.1595), a supporter of King Henry and Queen Margaret.

Exeter, Thomas Beaufort, Duke of

Historical but minor character in *Henry*

VI Part 1 (*c*.1592) and *Henry V* (*c*.1599). Exeter is the illegitimate son of John of Gaunt and the younger brother of the Bishop of Winchester, and later appears as the uncle of Henry V. His role is small and he has no particular personality.

Exton, Sir Piers

The murderer of *Richard II* (*c*.1597), together with a group of hired assassins, who accost the deposed King in his cell in Pomfret Castle. His small role is obviously of great importance.

F

Fabian

A member of Countess Olivia's household in *Twelfth Night* (1602), Fabian is part of the riotous crew consisting of Sir Toby Belch, Sir Andre Aguecheek, Maria, and Feste. Fabian is possibly a servant, but his position is not clear; his is a small but colourful role.

Fairy

Any of several minor characters in *A Midsummer Night's Dream* (1598) who, ideally, should be diminutive.

Falstaff, Sir John

Shakespeare's greatest comic character, Sir John is found in *Henry IV Parts 1 and 2* (1598/1600) and *The Merry Wives of Windsor* (*c*.1597). In the first two the setting is medieval, but in the last, more farce than history play, it is Elizabethan; this may reflect the haste with which the play is thought to have been written. In the Henry plays, Falstaff functions almost as a surrogate father for Hal, the riotous Prince of Wales. Falstaff is physically obese, amoral, cowardly and a thief, but in every sense larger-than-life. His irresponsible lifestyle is something which Prince Hal must give up in order to mature into his duties as the future monarch.

Falstaff is a witty rascal and although he has faults, some very serious faults in Part 2, he is nevertheless a very sympathetic stage character and one who is always popular with the audience. The vitality and energy of the characterisation is enormous, but a careful reading of Part 2 suggests that he is at least 70. In Part 2, the author begins his preparation for killing off Falstaff, by referring repeatedly to his failing health and to his age. In the final moments of Part 2, Falstaff and the young King meet. When Falstaff addresses the King familiarly, the latter's stern rebuff breaks the old man's heart.

I know thee not, old man. Fall to thy prayers.
How ill white hairs become a fool and jester!
I have long dreamt of such a kind of man,
So surfeit-swelled, so old, and so profane;
But being awake, I do despise my dream.

In *Henry V* (*c*.1599), although Falstaff does not appear, there is a very poignant description of his death. In *The Merry Wives of Windsor* (*c*.1597) Falstaff is the central character and his personality is entirely consistent with that in the histories. It is in the nature of farce that characterisation is less fully developed, however, and Falstaff is no exception. He is easily tricked several times by the

Herbert Beerbohm Tree plays Falstaff, one of his most famous roles, *c*.1902.

virtuous, middle-class housewives, Mrs Ford and Mrs Page.

The histories and the farce have always been popular. Falstaff is said to have been played in Shakespeare's company by John Lowin, John Heminge (editor of the First Folio), and William Hart, the author's nephew. The great actor Thomas Betterton was a notable Falstaff in the Restoration period, while in the eighteenth century James Quin and John Henderson were notable impersonators. David Garrick played the role, but it was not one of his best characters. In the nineteenth century both Steven and Charles Kemble took the part, while Charles Bartley made a career of it between 1815 and 1852. In the twentieth century there have been many well-reviewed performances, but Sir Ralph Richardson's was particularly outstanding.

Fang
A small part in *Henry IV Part 2* (1600), a constable who tries to arrest Falstaff for debt.

Fastolfe, Sir John
Historical figure in *Henry VI Part 1* (*c*.1592), a cowardly English soldier whose role is marginal.

Father that hath killed his Son, the
A nameless soldier in *Henry VI Part 3* (*c*.1595) who prepares to loot a corpse at the Battle of Towton, only to find it is his own son. The corollary is the Son that hath killed his Father. Both symbolic incidents are witnessed by Henry VI, who has withdrawn from the battle to meditate and is deeply distressed by the sorrow of civil war.

Faulconbridge, Lady
A minor character in *King John* (*c*.1595), mother of a major character, Philip Faulconbridge, known as the Bastard, and a minor character, Robert Faulconbridge.

Faulconbridge, Philip
See 'Bastard, the'.

Faulconbridge, Robert
Minor character in *King John* (*c*.1595), the legitimate son of Lady Faulconbridge by her husband.

Faulconbridge, Wiliam Neville, Lord
Minor walk-on mentioned in *Henry VI Part 3* (*c*.1595), sometimes assigned the lines of Montague.

Feeble, Francis
Minor character in *Henry IV Part 2* (1600) whom Falstaff recruits for the King's army.

Fenton, Master
A secondary character in *The Merry Wives of Windsor* (*c*.1597), who functions in the sub-plot of the wooing of Anne Page. As he is a presentable young man, she prefers him to the other two, who are misfits, and so she elopes with him.

Ferdinand
The young man who gains the love of Miranda, Prospero's daughter, in *The Tempest* (1611). Ferdinand is the son of Prospero's old enemy, King Alonso of Naples.

Ferdinand, King of Navarre
The ruling authority in *Love's Labour's Lost* (*c*.1598). His decision to eschew the company of ladies and all revelry for a lengthy period of scholarship is the guiding idea which sets the comedy in motion, but he succumbs to the charm and intelligence of the Princess of France. His character is rather one-dimensional.

Feste
A jester in the household of Countess Olivia in *Twelfth Night* (1602), who also frequents the court of her neighbour, and rejected suitor, Count Orsino. Feste's songs add greatly to the atmosphere of this romantic comedy.

Fidele
The name taken by Imogen, the heroine of *Cymbeline* (1611), when she is in disguise as a youth.

Fiend
Any of several supernatural beings linked to Joan la Pucelle (Joan of Arc) in *Henry VI Part 1* (*c.*1592).

First Murderer
One of several very small parts in *Henry VI Part 2* (*c.*1594), the killers of the Duke of Gloucester.

First Murderer
One of two hired killers in *Richard III* (*c.*1597), who act on orders from the future *Richard III* (*c.*1597) to kill his brother, Clarence, in the Tower of London. This is a key crime by the title character.

First Murderer
Minor character in *Macbeth* (1606).

Fishermen
Three minor characters in *Pericles, Prince of Tyre* (*c.*1609).

Fitzwater, Lord Walter
Minor historical character in *Richard II* (*c.*1597), who is a supporter of Henry Bolingbroke.

Flaminius
Servant of the title character in *Timon of Athens* (*c.*1604).

John Laurie as Feste, 1932.

Nickolas Grace plays Florizel to Cherie Lunghi's Perdita, 1976.

Flavius
Steward in the household of the title character in *Timon of Athens c.*1604).

Flavius (L. Caesetius Flavus)
Minor historical character in *Julius Caesar* (1599) who is a Roman tribune and an ally of Brutus.

Fleance
A minor character in *Macbeth* (1606), this youth is the son of Banquo and, unlike his father, escapes Macbeth's murderers.

Florence, Duke of
A courtly ruler and minor figure in *All's Well That Ends Well* (*c.*1603).

Florizel
The romantic young prince in the second part of *The Winter's Tale* (1611), who is a suitor to the supposed shepherd girl Perdita. He is a typical young lover, with little personality.

Fluellen, Captain
A Welsh officer in the army of *Henry V* (*c.*1599).

Flute, Francis
One of the 'rude mechanicals' in *A Midsummer Night's Dream* (1598), who rehearse and perform a play for the Duke's wedding. Flute is a workman whose trade is bellows-mender.

Follower

Any one of several walk-ons led by Laertes in *Hamlet* (*c*.1602).

Fool

An important secondary character in *King Lear* (1608). The fool is a court jester to Lear; he is wise, and tries to guide his elderly master and cheer him as his mind begins to fail. The fool is with King Lear in the traumatic storm scene, but then disappears from the play.

Fool

Minor character, a jester in *Timon of Athens* (*c*.1604).

Ford, Mrs Alice

One of the two wives in *The Merry Wives of Windsor* (*c*.1597). She and her friend, Mrs Page, receive identical love letters from Sir John Falstaff and resolve to play tricks on him.

Peg Woffington as a famous eighteenth-century Mrs Ford.

Ford, Frank

A secondary character in *The Merry Wives of Windsor* (*c*.1597), Ford is the insanely jealous husband of Alice Ford, one of the 'merry wives'.

Fordham, John, Bishop of Ely

Minor figure in *Henry V* (*c*.1599) who supports the Archbishop of Canterbury in urging Henry to invade France.

Forester

Minor character in *Love's Labour's Lost* (*c*.1598).

Fortinbras

Minor character in *Hamlet* (*c*.1602), the King of Norway and an enemy of Denmark. He is a young warrior who appears late in the play to conclude the proceedings.

France, King of

Secondary character in *All's Well That Ends Well* (*c*.1603).

France, King of

Minor character in *King Lear* (1608) who weds Lear's younger daughter, Cordelia, without a dowry and takes her to France.

France, Princess of

The principal romantic heroine in *Love's Labour's Lost* (*c*.1598).

Francesca

A very minor character in *Measure For Measure* (1604), a nun.

Francis

Minor character in *Henry IV Parts 1 and 2* (1598/1600), who is a servant at the Boar's Head Tavern.

Francis, Friar

A minor character in *Much Ado About Nothing* (*c*.1599), who officiates at the disastrous marriage ceremony between Hero and Claudio.

Francisco

Minor character who is a sentry on duty on the ramparts in *Hamlet* (*c*.1602).

Francisco

Minor character in *The Tempest* (1611), a follower of King Alonso.

Frederick, Duke

The younger brother and deposer of Duke Senior in *As You Like It* (1600). The two Dukes are the fathers of the two heroines, Rosalind and Celia. Frederick is portrayed as a conventional villain.

French Soldier
A walk-on taken prisoner by Pistol in *Henry V* (c.1599).

Frenchman
A minor figure in *Cymbeline* (1611).

Friar
A small role in *Measure For Measure* (1604), he helps the Duke of Vienna with his disguise.

Friend
Either of two minor acquaintances of the gaoler in *The Two Noble Kinsmen* (c.1613).

Froth
A small character in *Measure For Measure* (1604), a customer in the bordello.

G

Gadshill
A minor character in *Henry IV Part 1* (1598), a robber and friend of Falstaff.

Gallus, Caius Cornelius
A follower of Caesar in *Antony and Cleopatra* (1608), who was a historical person.

Gamekeepers
Two extras in *Henry VI Part 3* (c.1595).

Ganymede
Name taken by Rosalind in *As You Like It* (1600) when in disguise as a youth.

Gaoler
A male custodian. Gaolers appear in *The Merchant of Venice* (c.1598); *Cymbeline* (1611); *The Winter's Tale* (1611); and *The Two Noble Kinsmen* (c.1613). A 'jailor' appears in *The Comedy of Errors* (c.1594).

Gardener
One of several in *Richard II* (c.1597) whose reflections on the unkempt state of England and the culpability of King Richard are unfortunately overheard by Richard's unhappy Queen.

Gardiner, Stephen
Minor historical character in *Henry VIII* (1613), a follower of Cardinal Wolsey and later Bishop of Winchester.

Gargrave, Sir Thomas
Minor historical character in *Henry VI Part 1* (c.1592), an officer who is killed in battle in France.

Garter (Garter King-at-Arms)
Minor functionary at court in *Henry VIII* (1613).

Gaunt, John of, Duke of Lancaster (1340-99)
An important historical figure who is a secondary character in *Richard II* (c.1597). He is the elderly uncle of the title character, and the father of Richard's adversary, Henry Bolingbroke. His death scene in Act II contains his sublime description of England:

This royal throne of kings, this sceptred isle,
This earth of majesty, this seat of Mars,
This other Eden, demi-paradise,
This fortress built by nature for herself
Against infection and the hand of war,
This happy breed of men, this little world,
This precious stone set in a silver sea,
Which serves it in the office of a wall,
Or as a moat defensive to a house
Against the envy of less happier lands;
This blessed plot, this earth, this realm, this
  England . . .

General
A walk-on in *Henry VI Part 1* (c.1592), a French officer.

Lionel Brough as a gardener in *Richard II*.

Gentleman

Walk-ons required in *Henry VI Part 2* (*c.*1594); *Richard III* (*c.*1597); *Hamlet* (*c.*1602); *All's Well That Ends Well* (1603): *Measure For Measure* (1604); *Othello* (1604); *King Lear* (1608); *Pericles, Prince of Tyre* (*c.*1609); *Cymbeline* (1611); *The Winter's Tale* (1611): *Henry VIII* (1613); and *The Two Noble Kinsmen* (*c.*1613).

Gentlewoman

A minor figure, attendant on Lady Macbeth in her famous 'sleepwalking scene' in *Macbeth* (1606).

Gentlewoman

Walk-on attendant to Volumnia and Virgilia in *Coriolanus* (*c.*1608).

Gertrude, Queen

A major figure in *Hamlet* (*c.*1602), Queen of Denmark and mother of the hero, whose love for her borders on the obsessional. As the tragedy opens, she is newly married to her brother-in-law, Claudius, who has succeeded to the throne of Hamlet's father. This marriage is looked upon as incestuous in the context of the play. Although it transpires that Claudius has murdered his brother, no guilt for that crime accrues to Gertrude. Her son charges her with excessive and unbecoming sexuality, in her hasty remarriage, which is the most that can be said against her. 'Frailty, thy name is woman', he says of his mother. The Queen dearly loves her son, and she shows a change of heart towards the evil Claudius after her son upbraids her. Ironically she dies by a poison cup which Claudius had intended for Hamlet.

Ghost

Shakespeare's audience loved ghosts and supernatural figures. In his virtuoso early play, *Richard III* (*c.*1597), he exploits this to the full by employing eleven minor but significant ghosts, who appear at the end of the play on the eve of the Battle of Bosworth Field. These represent the characters whom Richard has murdered in his ascent to the throne and they appear in the order in which they died. First come Edward, Prince of Wales, and his father, Henry VI, followed by Clarence, and the Lords Rivers, Grey and Vaughan. Next comes Lord William Hastings, followed by the two little Princes Edward and Richard, Richard III's wife Lady Anne, and lastly Buckingham. Each of these ghosts first appears in Richard's tent to curse him, and then crosses to Richmond's (the future Henry VII's) tent to bless him.

Ghost

The ghost of *Julius Caesar* (1599) is a good way of keeping his spirit to the forefront in the final scenes.

Ghost

The ghost of Hamlet's father is the spring which sets the plot of *Hamlet* (*c.*1602) in motion. The ghost makes two appearances in Act I. The first is silent, and the second contains his lengthy speech to his son about how he met his death. Much later the Ghost again appears to Hamlet, in his mother's closet or bedroom, but is invisible to her. Tradition has it that the Ghost was played by the author.

Ghost

Banquo, who has been murdered by agents of Macbeth appears at the banquet which is the central scene in *Macbeth* (1606) to haunt the title character, but is invisible to everyone else. The purpose of ghosts in tragedy is usually to call for revenge.

Constance Collier plays a haunted Gertrude, 1925.

Ghost
The family of Posthumus, the hero in *Cymbeline* (1611), appears to him in a dream, accompanied by music.

Girl (Margaret Plantagenet)
Historical but minor character in *Richard III* (c.1597). She is one of two children of the murdered Clarence, who by rights should be higher up the line of succession than their uncle, Richard.

Glasdale, Sir William
Historical but very minor figure in *Henry VI Part 1* (c.1592).

Glendower, Owen (c.1359-c.1416)
Historical figure found in *Henry IV Part 1* (1598). Glendower, although important historically, is only marginal in the play. A Welsh military leader who is opposed to Henry, Glendower interprets for Lady Mortimer, his daughter, who does not speak English, and whose husband does not speak Welsh. He is one of those characters in the histories whom Shakespeare delights in delineating by their regional backgrounds.

Gloucester, Eleanor Cobham, Duchess of
Historical character whom we meet in *Henry VI Part 2* (c.1594), and whose husband is heir apparent to King Henry. Her ambitious machinations lead to her downfall and that of her guileless husband, but her role is a secondary one.

Gloucester, Eleanor de Bohun, Duchess of
Historical character found in *Richard II* (c.1597). She is the sister-in-law of the King's celebrated uncle, John of Gaunt, but hers is a minor part.

Gloucester, Earl of
An important secondary character in *King Lear* (1608). Like the King, Gloucester is an elderly character who is abused by his offspring, and is unable to distinguish between his virtuous and villainous child.

The sub-plot of Gloucester's relationship with his two sons parallels the main plot of Lear and his three daughters. The Earl is loyal to Lear, which leads to his blinding by one of Lear's daughters and her wicked husband. This stage business is extremely powerful and unpleasant, but the blinding of Gloucester and Lear's loss of his reason are symbolic of their spiritual state, which is one of lack of awareness. This is brought out when the two old friends meet on the beach at Dover, one blind and the other mad. This is a most touching scene; their recognition of each other and of their mutual suffering continues the climb to the tragic catharsis which causes many people, including Bernard Shaw, to consider this Shakespeare's greatest play.

Gloucester, Humphrey, Duke of (1390-1447)
Historical figure in *Henry VI Parts 1 and 2* (c.1592/c.1594)), *Henry IV Part 2* (1600), and *Henry V* (c.1599). Duke Humphrey is the youngest son of Henry IV and brother of Henry V. In *Henry VI* he is Lord Protector on behalf of the young King, Henry VI. He is presented as the main reason for England's loss of the Hundred Years' War with France, and he becomes controversial, as does his wife, Eleanor Cobham. She is banished; he is executed, falsely charged with treason.

The Penance of the Duchess of Gloucester, from Henry VI, Part 2.

Peter Geddis as Launcelot Gobbo with Gordon Gostelow as Old Gobbo, 1972.

Gobbo, Launcelot

A comic servant in *The Merchant of Venice* (*c.*1598), who has no particular character aside from his buffoonery.

Gobbo, Old

A minor character in *The Merchant of Venice* (*c.*1598), the nearly-blind father of the clown, Launcelot Gobbo.

Goneril

A leading character in *King Lear* (1608), Goneril is one of the elderly King's three daughters. She and her wicked sister, Regan, at first act in accord in attempting to curb their father, but gradually the two become enemies. Goneril is marginally more villainous than Regan, but has a virtuous husband, Albany, although he is a weak character. Both sisters lust after Edmund, the evil bastard son of the Duke of Gloucester; as a result of this rivalry, Goneril poisons Regan and then commits suicide. The two sisters need to be clearly distinguished in casting, as they are so alike in the writing.

Estelle Kohler as Goneril with Ralph Fiennes as Edmund, 1990.

Gonzalo

A secondary character in *The Tempest* (1611), who is in the train of King Alonso of Naples. Gonzalo is an older man whose nature is kindly.

Goths

Several walk-ons in *Titus Andronicus* (*c.*1594), supporters of the title character.

Gough, Michael

A minor character in *Henry VI Part 2* (*c.*1594) who loses his life in the Cade rebellion.

Governor of Harfleur

Minor French official in *Henry V* (*c.*1599).

Governor of Paris

Minor French official in *Henry VI Part 1* (*c.*1592).

Gower

Messenger in *Henry IV Part 2* (1600).

Gower, Captain

Minor character in *Henry V* (*c.*1599), an officer in Henry's army.

Gower, John (*c.*1330-1408)

Historical figure, a writer and friend of Chaucer, who is a secondary character in *Pericles, Prince of Tyre* (*c.*1609), where he is called the Presenter and functions as a choral figure, speaking introductory passages before several scenes. John Gower's main work was *Confessio Amantis* (1390), which is the chief source used by Shakespeare and his unknown collaborator in *Pericles*.

Grandpré

A minor French nobleman in *Henry V* (*c.*1599).

Gratiano

A secondary character in *The Merchant of Venice* (*c.*1598), Gratiano is a Venetian, but something of a 'rough diamond'. He is a friend of the hero, Bassanio, and marries Portia's maid, Nerissa, in a double wedding with Bassanio and Portia. He is thus one of the three sets of lovers with which this romantic comedy deals.

Gratiano
A very marginal character in *Othello* (1604), a Venetian nobleman and uncle of the heroine, Desdemona.

Greene, Henry
Minor historical figure in *Richard II* (c.1597) who, together with Bagot and Bushy, is a less than admirable follower of Richard.

Gregory
Servant of the Capulet family in *Romeo and Juliet* (1597).

Gremio
Elderly suitor of the lovely Bianca in *The Taming of the Shrew* (c.1594). Shakespeare calls him a 'pantaloon' a character type from commedia dell'arte who is depicted as a greedy old man.

Grey, Sir Richard
A relative of Queen Elizabeth in *Richard III* (c.1597), a minor figure who is executed by Richard's orders.

Grey, Thomas
A minor character in *Henry V* (c.1599) who is part of a plot to kill the King. This historical traitor was executed by the young King prior to his departure for his French campaign.

Griffith
A minor functionary in *Henry VIII* (1613) who is the official escort, or gentleman usher, of Queen Katharine at her trial.

Groom
Supporter of the King in *Richard II* (c.1597).

Groom
Any of three walk-ons who strew the streets with rushes prior to the coronation of Henry V in *Henry IV Part 2* (1600). Some editions call them 'strewers'.

Grumio
Comic servant of Petruchio in *The Taming of the Shrew* (c.1594). Like many similar characters in Shakespeare, he is derived from Roman comic types.

Guardsman
Any of several walk-ons in *Antony and Cleopatra* (1608) who are subordinates of the hero.

Guardsman
Any of several walk-ons in *Antony and Cleopatra* (1608) who are subordinates of Octavius Caesar.

Guiderius
A young man in *Cymbeline* (1611), also known as Polydore, who, with his brother, proves to the the long-lost son of the King, and is restored to Cymbeline at the end. Guiderius is brave and keen, and helps to defeat the invading Roman forces.

Guildenstern
A minor character in *Hamlet* (c.1602) who, together with his friend Rosencrantz, was a fellow student with Prince Hamlet at Wittenberg University before the play opens. Gradually, however, the two men become evil dupes of King Claudius. Hamlet, discovering their perfidy, connives to send them to their doom.

Guildford, Sir Henry
An actual person but minor character in *Henry VIII* (1613), where he functions as a steward to Cardinal Wolsey.

Gurney, James
Servant of Lady Faulconbridge in *King John* (c.1595), a virtually silent figure.

H

Haberdasher, The
A tradesman in *The Taming of the Shrew* (c.1594).

Halberdier

Walk-on who appears in *Richard III* (*c*.1597), accompanying the coffin of Henry VI, and in Henry VIII (1613).

Hamlet

The title character in what many regard as Shakespeare's greatest play, his tragedy *Hamlet, Prince of Denmark* (*c*.1602). Hamlet is an introspective and melancholy young man when we first meet him, and he is dressed in black in mourning for his father, the late King Hamlet. Obsessively devoted to his mother, Queen Gertrude, Hamlet has been strongly alienated by her hasty re-marriage to his uncle, which is seen as incestuous. Oedipal interpretations of Hamlet's response to his mother have been a feature of some modern productions, but his grief for his father is equally acute.

Hamlet is a psychologically complex character even before he becomes aware that his hated uncle, King Claudius, has murdered his father. The ghost of Hamlet's father urges his son to revenge, but Hamlet delays carrying this out. Catching his uncle at prayer, Hamlet passes up the opportunity to kill him, for fear his uncle's praying soul will go to heaven. This desire to damn even his soul was seen by the great eighteenth-century critic, Dr Johnson, as deeply shocking in Shakespeare. Part of Hamlet's subsequent progress towards his own salvation is his gradual recognition of his own capacity for evil.

Confronting his mother in her quarters, Hamlet accidentally and in a rage stabs the courtier Polonius, who is hiding behind the arras. Hamlet's attitude towards the death of the father of his former love, Ophelia, is at first callous, although he later regrets the death of Polonius. His action, however, leads to the insanity and death of Ophelia, whom he has rejected in his extreme aversion to sex, brought on by his mother's re-marriage. Hamlet's killing of the innocent Polonius also results in the Prince's banishment from Denmark, during which his view of life becomes more philosophical and resigned.

The American comic playwright, George S. Kaufman, is supposed to have said that the problem with *Hamlet* was that it had too many quotations! Certainly it is an unusually long play, and unusually rich in celebrated passages. A particular problem with *Hamlet* is that it alone in the canon has three early texts; Quarto 1 (1603); Quarto 2 (1604); and the longest text, the First Folio (1623). Even Hamlet's soliloquies are not entirely consistent within these options, but we may refer briefly to each:

O that this too too solid (sullied) flesh would melt,
Thaw, and resolve itself into a dew,
Or that the Everlasting had not fixed
His canon 'gainst self-slaughter. O God! God!

ACT I, SC. 2

O, what a rogue and peasant slave am I!

ACT II, SC. 2

To be, or not to be; that is the question:
Whether 'tis nobler in the mind to suffer
The slings and arrows of outrageous fortune,
Or to take arms against a sea of troubles,
And, by opposing, end them . . .

ACT III, SC. I

How all occasions do inform against me,
And spur my dull revenge. What is a man
If his chief good and market of his time
Be but to sleep and feed? A beast, no more.

ACT IV, SC. 4

Harley Granville-Barker has called attention to the 'journey motif' which repeatedly informs the dramatic structure of *Hamlet*, and indeed at least sixteen journeys are part of the story, but the over-riding journey is that of Hamlet himself to self-awareness and salvation. In accepting his fate and impending death, Hamlet reassures his friend, Horatio (in prose):

Not a whit. We defy augury. There's a special providence in the fall of a sparrow. If it be now, 'tis not to come; if it be not to come, it will be now; if it be not now, yet it will come.

The readiness is all. Since no man, of aught he leaves, knows aught, what is't to leave betimes. Let be.

ACT V, SC. 2

Hamlet begs pardon of Laertes for killing the latter's father, Polonius. A final grace note is sounded by Horatio over Hamlet's dead body.

Now cracks a noble heart. Good night, sweet prince,
And flights of angels sing thee to thy rest.

ACT V, SC. 2

The character of Hamlet has taken on mythic qualities. He is universally regarded as one of the greatest characters in literature, and each performance seems to re-invent the character for its own age. Almost certainly the part was created by Richard Burbage at the Globe Theatre, with the author as the Ghost. David Garrick took the part between 1734 and 1776 and, beginning in 1783, John Philip Kemble established himself as one of the greatest of all Hamlets. His sister, Sarah Siddons, who acted both Ophelia and Gertrude opposite Kemble, also acted Hamlet herself, but never in London. Female Hamlets were popular in the late eighteenth century and throughout the nineteenth; examples are Kitty Clive, Charlotte Cushman and Sarah Bernhardt. Of the great Hamlets after Kemble, one must cite William Charles Macready, Edwin Booth, Henry Irving, Johnston Forbes-Robertson, John Barrymore, John Gielgud, Laurence Olivier and Kenneth Branagh. *Hamlet* has been filmed at least 25 times, and numerous foreign language productions have been staged over the centuries.

ABOVE LEFT Hamlet, by C. Walter Hodges.
ABOVE Mel Gibson as Hamlet with Alan Bates as Claudius in the 1990 film.
BELOW LEFT The play scene in *Hamlet* by Daniel Maclise.
BELOW RIGHT Edwin Booth as Hamlet, 1864.

Harcourt
Messenger in *Henry IV Part 2* (1600).

Harpy
Supernatural guise in which Ariel appears in *The Tempest* (1611).

Hastings
Official in *Richard III* (*c.*1597).

Hastings, Lord Randolph
Historical character in *Henry IV Part 2* (1600), whose role is marginal; he is a rebel against King Henry.

Hastings, Lord William
This historical character is found in *Henry VI Part 3* (*c.*1595) and in *Richard III* (*c.*1597). Hastings supports the Yorkist cause and is a somewhat more important figure in the later play.

Hecate
A minor character in *Macbeth* (1606), Hecate is an evil spirit who is associated with the three main witches.

Hector
Legendary figure who features in *Troilus and Cressida* (*c.*1603), the heroic Hector is a prince of Troy and brother of Troilus.

Helen
The legendary Helen of Troy (actually Helen, Queen of Sparta) appears as a secondary character in *Troilus and Cressida* (*c.*1603). Well before the play opens, the Trojan prince, Paris, has stolen Helen from her husband, King Menelaus, causing the Trojan War. She only appears in one scene of Shakespeare's play, and he depicts her as a silly woman.

Helen
Attendant on Imogen in *Cymbeline* (1611).

Helena
The heroine of *All's Well That Ends Well* (*c.*1603), Helena is the daughter of a famous physician, who has died and left her in the charge of the elderly Countess

Lily Brayton as Helena in *A Midsummer Night's Dream*, 1905.

of Rossillion. Helena loves Bertram, the Countess's son, but he does not return her love. She is able to cure the King of France of his fatal malady, with some secret prescriptions and potions left her by her father. As her reward she asks for Bertram's hand, but must resort to the notorious 'bed trick' to win his love, that is, substitute herself for another woman in his bed, thus inducing him to father her child. It is possible to read Helena as possessive and unscrupulous. On the other hand, she is a bright and resourceful young woman who loves a man unworthy of her. This central relationship gives rise to the difficulties which place this drama in the group of so-called 'problem plays'.

Helena
One of the two young heroines who get lost in the woods with their swains and are the subjects of pranks by the fairy, Puck, in *A Midsummer Night's Dream*

(1598). Helena and Hermia are school friends; the former is tall and fair, the latter short and dark. Both are good-natured, lively girls. Helena loves Demetrius, but Hermia's father is determined that Demetrius should marry Hermia.

Helenus

Legendary but minor figure in *Troilus and Cressida* (c.1603), a son of King Priam of Troy.

Helicanus

Minor character in *Pericles, Prince of Tyre* (c.1609) whom the title character leaves in charge of Tyre. Helicanus is a loyal counsellor of the Prince.

Henry, Prince, later King Henry III of England
(1207-72)

An historical but marginal character in *King John* (c.1595), whose son Henry is.

Henry IV, King of England
(1366-1413)

See Bolingbroke.

Henry V, King of England
(1387-1422)

One of the playwright's most vibrant characters, Henry is first found as the Prince of Wales, 'Prince Hal', the heir apparent in *Henry IV Parts 1 and 2* (1598/1600). Then he becomes the title character in the patriotic epic *Henry V* (c.1599). As the Prince, he is depicted sowing his wild oats with a group of riotous companions at the Boar's Head Tavern, including most notably the rascally Sir John Falstaff. Hal's wild ways are a source of great sorrow to his father, Henry IV, beset by political troubles and failing health. The picture of the irresponsible youth only serves to heighten the contrast, however, when Hal develops into a devout and conscientious King (see 'Bolingbroke', 'Falstaff').

In the play that bears his name, Henry having taken advice on the validity of his claim to the French throne, prepares for his invasion of France, which will culminate in the famous victory at Agincourt against vastly superior

Henry V and Falstaff, by C. Walter Hodges.

Richard Burton plays a young and solemn Henry V, 1951.

numbers. From the outset of the play, the young King amazes all and sundry with his Christian piety and his understanding of military and political matters. His stature as the 'mirror of all Christian kings' is evident from his very first scene, but is repeatedly reinforced, especially by his ability to handle men. Henry inspires his followers with two ringing orations.

Once more unto the breath, dear friends, once more,
Or close the wall up with our English dead.
In peace there's nothing so becomes a man
As modest stillness and humility.
But when the blast of war blows in our ears,
Then imitate the action of a tiger . . .
Follow your spirit, and upon this charge
Cry 'God for Harry! England and St. George!'

ACT III, SCENE 2

And Crispin Crispian shall ne'er go by
From this day to the ending of the world
But we in it shall be rememberèd,
We few, we happy few, we band of brothers.
For he today that sheds his blood with me
Shall be my brother; be he ne'er so vile,
This day shall gentle his condition.

ACT IV, SCENE 2

Henry is equally impressive in his quieter moments, such as his solitary prayer on the eve of the battle, and his incognito stroll among his disheartened troops at midnight. A man's man, his later wooing of the shy French princess finds him, for the one and only time, ill at ease. This completes the very human, although exceptional, characterisation of 'this star of England'. The author's chief sources are Raphael Holinshed's *Chronicles of England, Scotland and Ireland*, and Edward Hall's *The Union of the Two Noble and Illustrious Families of Lancaster And York*.

The stage history of the play prior to World War II was patchy. The only known performance in the seventeenth century was before James I in 1605. David Garrick produced *Henry V*, but did not play the King; John Philip Kemble, William Charles Macready and Charles Kean acted Henry, but followed Garrick in using adaptations. In recent times, the Royal Shakespeare Company, the BBC and others have tended to present the play as part of a cycle of the histories, and films of *Henry V*, that of Laurence Olivier in 1944 and Kenneth Branagh in 1989, have brought the play to huge audiences. These drastically different interpretations have both nevertheless been greatly loved, especially the earlier one. Both actors played the King on the stage, but the epic nature of the play has been more fully exploited by the cinema.

Henry VI, King of England
(1421-71)

The title character of Shakespeare's only trilogy is nevertheless not the leading character in *Henry VI Part 1* (*c*.1592), as he does not make his first appearance until Act III, Scene 1, and then is only a youth. England loses France, and Part 1 ends with the engagement of Henry to a captured French noblewoman, Margaret of Anjou, whom he has never seen. This proves to be a fatal error. Henry is gentle and pious, and his weakness and youth provide a power vacuum into which ambitious nobles, and Queen Margaret herself, plunge. The King becomes little more than a witness to the resurgence of the civil unrest between his own faction, the Lancasters, and his relatives, the Yorks, which had characterised the reign of his grandfather, Henry IV. Henry's cause is led in Parts 2 and 3 by the increasingly ruthless and unscrupulous Queen Margaret. King Henry is no leader of men, and his contemplative nature provides no effective check on the evil of those around him. He is unable to save his uncle and former guardian, Duke Humphrey of Gloucester, from their machinations.

Shakespeare's portrait of Henry VI is subtle. He is the quiet at the centre of the storm, and his character is probably more congenial to modern auditors than to previous ages; he alone has no desire for revenge. The author, of course, is greatly telescoping time in the trilogy, but even as Henry gets older, he becomes no more able to control events. In Part 3 he does try to end the growing civil war, but he cannot reconcile Margaret with the Yorks. Henry withdraws from the decisive battle of Towton to meditate, and witnesses the key scenes between the 'son that hath killed his father', and the 'father that hath killed his son'. These emblematic scenes symbolise the peculiar agony of civil war and totally depress Henry. Shakespeare alleges that Henry is murdered by the future Richard III, son of Richard, Duke of York. As Henry is

Alan Howard as Henry VI and Helen Mirren as Queen Margaret, 1978.

killed by the future tyrant, he prophesies the horrors that will ensue with Richard's reign. The final irony of Shakespeare's trilogy is that Henry's very virtues are his undoing.

The stage history of these plays has been very slight. *Henry VI Part 1* is recorded as having been produced before the theatres closed in 1592 and was a success, although it is not necessarily thought now that it was written before Parts 2 and 3. After that performance, however, all three parts were largely ignored, partly because of the distasteful portrait of Joan La Pucelle (Joan of Arc). Productions are recorded only in 1738 and 1899, although elements of the trilogy were sometimes used in abridgements. The trilogy has been much more popular in the twentieth century, especially in various cycles presented by the Royal Shakespeare Company, the BBC and, occasionally, other companies. Alan Howard gave a particularly impressive performance as Henry VI with the Royal Shakespeare Company, and on several occasions acted the entire trilogy on one day.

Henry VII, King of England (1457-1509)
See Richmond.

Henry VIII, King of England (1491-1547)
The title character in *Henry VIII* (1613), the author's last work for the theatre, which he co-authored with John Fletcher, according to expert opinion dating from the nineteenth century and largely endorsed today.

The story mainly concerns the trial of the king's first wife, Queen Katharine of Aragon, her subsequent divorce from the King, and his remarriage to Anne Boleyn. Henry is presented in a favourable light, as a ruler who grows in wisdom, but only a small part of his reign is dealt with in the play. The authors' chief source is Holinshed's *Chronicles*, but they give no hint of the later violent behaviour of this King. Here King Henry is a symbol of

Richard Griffiths plays Henry VIII, 1983.

England's greatness, one who leads the country to Protestantism. He personifies the Protestant cause, whereas Queen Katharine, although presented with great dignity and sympathy, represents the Catholic position. Wolsey, the only villain, is, of course, nominally Catholic; his downfall is poignantly linked to his redemption, and the play ends on a note of forgiveness and national renewal.

Sir William Davenant, said to be Shakespeare's godson, staged the play in 1664 with Thomas Betterton as King Henry, but this seems to have been an adaptation, as Samuel Pepys, who saw it, records in his diary that Henry appeared 'with all his wives'. From 1716, the actor-poet Colley Cibber staged it frequently, with Barton Booth as Henry. David Garrick staged many revivals with a great emphasis on spectacle, acting Henry opposite Hannah Pritchard as Katharine. Later, the play was associated with successive generations of the Kemble family of actors. The most elaborate production was probably that of Charles Kean in 1855. In the twentieth century, Henry has been acted by Charles Laughton, Anthony Quayle and Donald Sinden, among others.

Herald

A male figure acting as a messenger or official announcer. Heralds appear in *Henry VI Part 1* (*c*.1592); *Henry VI Part 2* (*c*.1594); *Richard II* (*c*.1597); *King John* (*c*.1595); *Henry V* (*c*.1599); *Othello* (1604); *King Lear* (1608); *Coriolanus* (*c*.1608); and *The Two Noble Kinsmen* (*c*.1613). Heralds add ceremony where appropriate, but are very small roles.

Herbert, Sir Walter

Minor historical character in *Richard III* (*c*.1597), an officer under Richmond.

Herbert, Sir William

Minor historical figure in *Henry VI Part 3* (*c*.1595) who is a supporter of Edward IV. Herbert is a silent figure.

Hermia

A major character in *A Midsummer Night's Dream* (1598), this energetic young lady is one of two heroines, the other being her friend Helena. Her father demands that Hermia be punished by the Duke for refusing to wed Demetrius. She instead elopes with Lysander, and the lovers are pursued by Demetrius and Helena. They all get lost in the enchanted woods where they become the butts of the magic of Puck, a fairy. The comic contrast between the two girls is a centrepiece of this popular comedy.

Hermione

This elegant and virtuous woman is the Queen of the jealous King Leontes in *The Winter's Tale* (1611). Hermione is unusual among Shakespearean heroines in that she is pregnant when we first meet her, and should be noticeably so. Wrongfully accused of adultery by the King, Hermione gives birth in prison (offstage) to the heroine of the second part of the play, Perdita. Hermione's high point in the play is her trial for adultery, where she eloquently defends her honour. Nevertheless her husband, King Leontes, sentences her to death, but their young son, Mamillius, dies suddenly and this diversion allows Paulina, a lady-in-waiting to the Queen, to secrete Hermione away from court, where she can be kept alive to figure in the play's happy ending 16 years later. Hermione is absent from the stage for a lengthy period in the centre of the story, and only reappears very briefly in the final moments, apparently miraculously resurrected from a statue. This has led some productions to cast one actress as Hermione/Perdita, such as Mary Anderson in 1887, as well as more recent performers. Notable Hermiones have been Sarah Siddons, Mrs Charles Kean (Ellen Tree), and Dame Judi Dench.

Mary Anderson as Hermione, 1887.

Hero

This rather bland young woman is a secondary character in *Much Ado About Nothing* (*c*.1599). She is the daughter of the Governor of Messina, and cousin of the more lively heroine, Beatrice. Hero is renounced at the altar by her betrothed, Claudio, who has been tricked into suspecting her of infidelity. Hero, who is shy and pliant, faints at the accusation. The plot which has slandered her is uncovered, however, and her reputation restored.

Hippolyta

A small but fanciful role in *A Midsummer Night's Dream* (1598), Hippolyta is the Queen of the Amazons. As the play opens, she is about to celebrate her nuptials to Theseus, the Duke of Athens. Shakespeare took their story from Chaucer's *The Knight's Tale*. There is not a great deal to her character, but she should be romantically appealing. As Hippolyta is absent from the stage for the whole centre section, some productions have doubled her role with Titania, the Queen of the Fairies. The purpose of this is not to save salaries, but to reinforce a directorial concept that the fairy tale which makes up the central action in the enchanted forest is actually the dream of Theseus and Hippolyta, to pass the time until their marriage.

Hippolyta

A character in *The Two Noble Kinsmen* (*c*.1613), Hippolyta, the Queen of the Amazons, appears first as the fiancée of Duke Theseus of Athens, and later as his wife.

Holland, John

Minor character in *Henry VI Part 2* (*c*.1594), a follower of the rebel, Jack Cade.

Holofernes

Minor character in *Love's Labour's Lost* (*c*.1598), a scholar. His pedantic character is almost incomprehensible, even more so to a modern audience, but the send-up of an 'egghead' is still funny.

Horatio

An important secondary character in *Hamlet* (*c*.1602). Horatio is a loyal friend of the melancholy hero, and the only person in the play whom Hamlet can confide in and, through Horatio, in the audience. Horatio was a school-fellow of the Prince, but otherwise we are told little of this calm young man; it is not clear if he is a Dane, or a foreigner.

Horner, Thomas

An armourer in *Henry VI Part 2* (*c*.1594).

Hortensio

Minor character in *The Taming of the Shrew* (*c*.1594), an unsuccessful suitor of Bianca. He has one very funny entrance where he comes on with a lute broken over his head, the result of an encounter with Bianca's shrewish older sister, Katherina.

Hortensius

Servant in *Timon of Athens* (*c*.1604).

Host

Walk-on figure in *The Two Gentlemen of Verona* (*c*.1598), an inn-keeper.

Host
Minor character in *The Merry Wives of Windsor* (*c*.1597), the jolly keeper of the Garter Tavern.

Hostess
Minor character in *The Taming of the Shrew* (*c*.1594). The hostess is proprietor of the tavern which is the setting for the induction scene.

Hostess
See Quickly, Mistress.

Hostilius
Minor character in *Timon of Athens* (*c*.1604), a visitor to the city.

Hotspur, Henry Percy (1364-1403)
An important historical figure in *Henry IV Part 1* (1598). He is a hot-headed youth who is noted for his military prowess, and is a rebel against Henry IV. Hotspur is a foil to Prince Hal, who is lethargic and dissolute in the company of his tavern companions, but Hal is ultimately inspired by Hotspur's example. The two young men meet in hand-to-hand combat at the Battle of Shrewsbury, where Prince Hal kills Hotspur. Hotspur's pride and impulsiveness are his undoing, but the author expands his character by giving him a loving wife, Lady Percy. He is introduced as a boy, known as Young Percy, in *Richard II* (*c*.1597), where his role is very marginal. Hotspur has been played by many leading actors, including Thomas Betterton, David Garrick, John Philip Kemble, William Charles Macready, and Laurence Olivier.

Hubert de Burgh
A small part in *King John* (*c*.1595), Hubert is the custodian of the young Prince Arthur and a follower of King John. He disobeys the King's order to kill Arthur, but the boy dies in an escape attempt.

H. Marston as Hotspur with F. Robinson as Prince Henry.

Hume, Sir John

Minor historical character in *Henry VI Part 2* (*c*.1594). Hume is a profane priest who plots with the witch Margery Jourdain and two sorcerers, on behalf of the Duchess of Gloucester.

Huntsman

Attendant of the captive Edward IV in *Henry VI Part 3* (*c*.1595).

Huntsman

Either of two walk-ons in the induction to *The Taming of the Shrew* (*c*.1594).

Hymen

A mythical figure, the Roman god of marriage, who rather oddly appears in the final moments of the otherwise realistic *As You Like It* (1600). Hymen is a masque-like character who functions as a '*deus ex machina*,' in a last-minute appearance which wraps up the strands of the plot. He presents the heroine, Rosalind, now out of her male disguise and ready to be reunited with her father. Four couples are to be wed at the conclusion, and Hymen blesses them. It is not clear whether Shakespeare intends Hymen to be a supernatural character, or someone whom Rosalind has set up.

Hymen

The Roman god of marriage appears as a silent figure in *The Two Noble Kinsmen* (*c*.1613), at the wedding of Theseus and Hippolyta.

I

Iachimo

An Italian gentleman and secondary character in *Cymbeline* (1611). Iachimo is a worldly and somewhat affected villain who pretends to have seduced the heroine, Imogen, in order to win a wager. He emerges from a trunk in her bedroom and steals a bracelet from the arm of the sleeping woman to prove his carnal knowledge of her. His supposed

Henry Irving as Iachimo with Ellen Terry as Imogen, 1896.

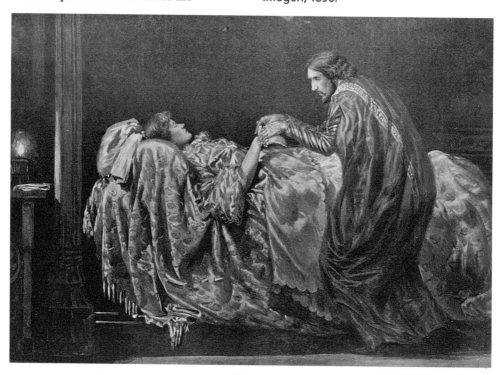

seduction puts Imogen's banished husband, Posthumus, into a towering jealousy. Iachimo has been linked to the figure of Iago, in *Othello* (1604), because both men are villains who spread lies about a recently-married and innocent woman, for seemingly very little reason. Iachimo's name is a diminutive of Iago, but the latter's villainy is far more sinister. Iachimo confesses his crime, and *Cymbeline*, in common with all the late romances, ends in reconciliation, with Posthumus forgiving Iachimo. The role of Iachimo was acted by Sir Henry Irving, with Ellen Terry as Imogen, at his Lyceum Theatre in 1896, a year after he became the first actor to be knighted.

Iago

A leading role in *Othello* (1604), Iago is one of Shakespeare's greatest creations. Iago's utter malevolence has challenged directors, actors and scholars down the ages to their uttermost, but no entirely satisfactory explanation has been advanced for his 'motiveless malignity', to use the famous phrase of Samuel Taylor Coleridge. Iago's is a long role; he is rarely absent from the stage for longer than 15 minutes at a stretch, and usually not that. In the manner of a tragic hero, he has several lengthy soliloquies. In these speeches he is quite frank with the audience about his perfidy and even gloats in it, to the point that the audience begins to laugh every time they hear him referred to as 'honest Iago', a frequent phrase on the lips of other characters. His relentless hostility and delight in evil makes him in one sense a stock machiavel character.

We are given one reasonable explanation for Iago's evil in the very first lines of the play, namely that he has been passed over for promotion by his commander, Othello. Later, in a soliloquy, he gives his other reasons.

The Moor – how be 't that I endure him not –
Is of a constant, loving, noble nature,
And I dare think he'll prove to Desdemona
A most dear husband. Now I do love her, too,

Laurence Olivier plays Iago, 1937-38.

Not out of absolute lust – though peradventure
I stand accountant for as great a sin –
But partly led to diet my revenge
For that I do suspect the lusty Moor
Hath leapt into my seat, the thought whereof
Doth, like a poisonous mineral, gnaw my inwards;
And nothing can or shall content my soul
Till I am evened with him, wife for wife.

Iago's wife Emilia, however, specifically denies adultery with Othello. The remaining reasons, Iago's jealousy of the goodness of Othello and Cassio, and his resentment at being passed over, are not sufficient to explain the enormity of his evil. The interpretation imposed by some directors, that Iago has a homosexual love for Othello, is very difficult to justify from lines in the text.

One possible solution, which can be supported from the text, is that Iago represents the presence of evil in the world, which cannot be explained unless it be by a religious dimension. That he is actually a devil, an agent of Satan, is hard for the modern auditor to accept, but Shakespeare's audience was still familiar with the tradition of medieval drama with its 'Vice' figure. The struggle in the old morality plays was between the Good and Bad Angel for the soul of man. In this context, Iago is the Bad Angel, whose power is only possible as a function of Othello's weakness. Desdemona is Othello's Good Angel. In one of his soliloquies Iago says:

> Divinity of hell:
> When devils will the blackest sins put on,
> They do suggest at first with heavenly shows,
> As I do now.

In conversation with his dupe, Roderigo, Iago says 'I am not what I am', and elsewhere he claims as his allies 'all the tribe of hell'. Most significantly, in his final conversation with Othello after the death of Desdemona, Othello refers to the tradition that devils were believed to have cloven feet and could not be killed.

Othello
I look down towards his feet, but that's a
  fable.
If that thou beest a devil I cannot kill thee.
(He wounds Iago)

Iago does not deny this charge, indeed he seems to accept it when he answers:

Iago
I bleed, sir, but not killed.
Othello
Will you, I pray, demand that demi-devil
Why he hath thus ensnared my soul and body.
Iago
Demand me nothing. What you know, you
  know.
From this time forth I never will speak word.

Those are his last words, and he is not killed within the text of the play. Of course Iago is no allegorical vice personified; he is a very realistically drawn character, except for the inexplicable degree of evil in him. But the references to hell, devils, damnation and the like reflect a strong line of imagery. Iago has been played by Charles Macklin, Charles Kean, William Charles Macready and Edwin Forrest, and in 1881 Henry Irving and Edwin Booth alternated Iago and Othello in London, with Ellen Terry as Desdemona. In the twentieth century,

one of the most noteworthy interpretations was a studio production by the Royal Shakespeare Company, with Sir Ian McKellen as Iago.

Iden, Alexander
Historical figure and minor character in *Henry VI Part 2* (c.1594), who kills the rebel Jack Cade.

Imogen
The heroine of *Cymbeline* (1611), Imogen is a 'breeches part'; she goes into disguise as a youth and spends part of the play in male attire. She is the daughter of King Cymbeline and the wife of Posthumus, whose love she loses through no fault of her own. She serves as page unknowingly to her own long-lost brothers, and then falls into the the hands of an invading Roman army. As the central figure in one of the author's late romances, her tale is utterly unbelievable, but her charm shines through and she is finally reunited with her father and her husband. In the nineteenth century, Imogen was associated with Helen Faucit, Adelaide Neilson and Ellen Terry, the latter widely acclaimed as the definitive Imogen. In 1957, Dame Peggy Ashcroft played the role at Stratford.

Interpreter
A French soldier in *All's Well That Ends Well* (c.1603).

Iras
The lesser of the two female attendants on the Queen of Egypt in *Antony and Cleopatra* (1608).

RIGHT Harriet Walter as Imogen accused by Nicholas Farrell's Posthumus, 1987.

Iris
One of three classical goddesses who appear in the masque in *The Tempest* (1611), Iris functions as the Presenter.

Isabel, Queen of England (1389-1409)
Although a small part, Queen Isabel is the leading female role in *Richard II* (*c.*1597), and is Richard's consort. She is a gentle, young Frenchwoman whom the King genuinely loves. Her most important moment is the symbolic scene where, with her ladies, she overhears the gardeners talking about Richard's woes, and likely deposition. Later, King and Queen are forcibly separated and she is sent back to France.

Isabel, Queen of France (1370-1435)
This very minor character appears briefly at the end of *Henry V* (*c.*1599) to bless the impending marriage of the English King with her daughter, Katherine.

Isabella
The leading female character in *Measure For Measure* (1604), Isabella, when we first meet her, is a novice in the Poor Clare order of nuns. She is diverted from her vocation to help her imprisoned brother, Claudio, and in so doing finds her virginity under threat from Angelo, the ranking civil authority in Vienna during the Duke's temporary absence. Although she is unquestionably an admirable and virtuous young lady, modern audiences tend to question her extreme position in holding that her virginity is more precious than her brother's life. Her attitudes become less rigid as the play progresses, and a solution is found by conniving with Mariana, a former love of Angelo, that she shall take the place of Isabella in Angelo's bed. The Duke, who has kept in touch with events during his absence, marries Isabella, who has learned a bit more tolerance. A flawed character, Isabella is nevertheless one of the author's more interesting young women characters.

Josette Simon as Isabella, 1987.

Isidore's Servant
A walk-on in *Timon of Athens* (*c.*1604).

J

Jailer
Minor character in *The Comedy of Errors* (*c.*1594).

Jamy, Captain
Minor character in *Henry V* (*c.*1599), a Scottish officer.

Jaquenetta
Minor figure in *Love's Labour's Lost* (*c.*1598), this sprightly country wench becomes pregnant by an affected braggart, Don Adriano de Armado.

Ruby Wax as Jaquenetta, 1979.

Jaques

An important secondary character in *As You Like It* (1600), Jaques is a morose and philosophical follower of the exiled Duke in the Forest of Arden. His most famous passage begins:

> All the world's a stage,
> And all the men and women merely players.
> They have their exits and their entrances,
> And one man in his time plays many parts,
> His acts being seven ages . . .

Jaques de Boys

Minor character in *As You Like It* (1600), the brother of the wicked Oliver and the young hero, Orlando. He makes his only appearance in Act V.

Jessica

This adventurous young lady is a secondary character in *The Merchant of Venice* (*c*.1598). Jessica is the daughter of the Jewish usurer Shylock, the leading character. Her boldness is indicated by her elopement with a Christian, Lorenzo, but her treatment of her father is fairly ruthless; she steals money from him, and also a ring her dead mother had given to him. Hers is another 'breeches part', in that she furthers her elopement by going into male disguise. Modern audiences may find her very abrupt abandonment of her religion part of the distasteful anti-Semitism which pervades the play.

Jessica and Shylock, after a painting by Gilbert Stuart Newton.

Jeweller

Minor character in *Timon of Athens* (*c*.1604).

Joan la Pucelle (Joan of Arc) (*c*.1412-31)

An important secondary character in *Henry VI Part 1* (*c*.1592). St Joan was not canonised until the twentieth century, and to the English of Shakespeare's day and earlier she was anything but a heroine. Nevertheless, it comes as a shock to a modern auditor to find her depicted as a whore and one who consorts with devils. She is the leader of the French army in the Hundred Years' War, and in her lifetime was known as La Pucelle, a name which the author takes from the *Chronicles*. Since it means 'the virgin', it is obviously inconsistent with the young Shakespeare's stage version of her, which is both debauched and historically inaccurate. She is shown fighting on the stage, and although this would have presented no problem for the boy actors at the Globe Theatre, it does pose problems for a modern actress.

John

Followers of Jack Cade in *Henry VI Part 2* (*c*.1594).

John

Walk-on servant in *The Merry Wives of Windsor* (*c*.1597).

John, Friar

The less important of the two friars who befriend the hero in *Romeo and Juliet* (1597); his role is marginal.

John, King of England (1167-1216)

The title character of the early history *King John* (*c*.1595). This protagonist is not entirely successful as a stage character, since he is neither hero nor villain. King John has usurped the throne from his nephew, Prince Arthur, but this theme lacks the vitality which we find in other usurpations such as that in *Richard II* (*c*.1597) and *Macbeth* (1606). King

Julia

The lesser of the two heroines in *The Two Gentlemen of Verona* (*c*.1598), Julia is a 'breeches part'. She disguises herself as a boy in order to follow Proteus, one of the title characters, with whom she is in love but who proves false. Like all of Shakespeare's breeches parts, Julia is independent and resourceful.

Juliet

Shakespeare's immortal heroine in *Romeo and Juliet* (1597). Juliet is the beautiful young daughter of a Veronese family. At the tender age of fourteen, her domineering father Capulet elects to marry her against her will to a personable young man, Paris. Instead she meets and falls in love with Romeo, who comes in disguise to a masked ball which her father is hosting. The first meeting of the lovers is couched in dialogue which forms a sonnet, but their two love scenes on her balcony are more celebrated. In the first balcony scene, Juliet says to Romeo:

My bounty is as boundless as the sea,
My love as deep. The more I give to thee
The more I have, for both are infinite.

BELOW Mary Anderson plays Juliet.

ABOVE Emrys James as a repentant King John with Jeffrey Dench as Cardinal Pandulph, 1975.

John's fortunes involve him in conflicts with his barons and the French, and he is finally poisoned by a monk. The author's picture of him is distorted and inaccurate, but the play is more concerned with power politics than personality.

Joseph

A servant of Petruchio in *The Taming of the Shrew* (*c*.1594).

Jourdain, Margery

This marginal character is a witch in *Henry VI Part 2* (*c*.1594); a historical figure, she was burned at the stake.

The extreme youth of Juliet is emphasised by the presence of her Nurse who, more than her mother Lady Capulet, is the heroine's friend and companion. Juliet's youth makes it all the more remarkable that she displays the strength to resist her parents, enter into a frightening plot with the Friar to evade their wishes, and ultimately take her own life. Her stature as a tragic heroine is indicated by Shakespeare's assigning to Juliet three soliloquies, the last two of which are extremely long, complex and highly dramatic. A justly famous lyrical passage from one of the soliloquies reads:

Come, gentle night; come, loving, black-
  browed night,
Give me my Romeo, and when he shall die,
Take him and cut him out in little stars,
And he will make the face of heaven so fine
That all the world will be in love with night,
And pay no worship to the garish sun.

This tragedy has always been popular. Fanny Kemble's stage debut as Juliet in 1829 was so sensational that it saved her father's theatre, Covent Garden, from bankruptcy. She continued to act the play with Charles Kemble for many years, both in Britain and America. Later, such stars as Ellen Terry, Julia Marlowe, Katherine Cornell, Peggy Ashcroft and

BELOW Johnston Forbes-Robertson and Mrs Patrick Campbell as the lovers, 1895.
ABOVE Olivia Hussey as Juliet in Zeffirelli's film, 1968.

Claire Bloom had successes as Juliet on both sides of the Atlantic. There have been many disasters, however; the difficulty is in casting an actress who is reasonably convincing as a fourteen-year-old, and yet able to cope with the high emotion of the role, and the intense vocal requirements of Juliet's speeches.

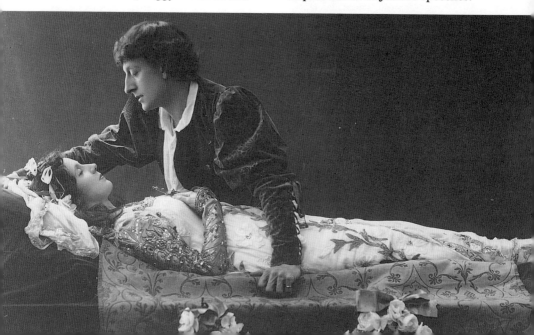

Juliet

This very small part is nevertheless essential to the plot of *Measure For Measure* (1604). Juliet is the betrothed of the hero, Claudio, who is imprisoned and placed under sentence of death for getting her pregnant. This is the circumstance upon which the plot hinges, although Juliet is a sketchy character, who only appears briefly in three scenes.

Juno

One of three classical goddesses who perform in the marriage masque in *The Tempest* (1611).

Jupiter

The supreme Roman god who appears in a vision to Posthumus in *Cymbeline* (1611) as, quite literally, a '*deus ex machina*' (god from the machine), a last-minute structural device which ties up untidy endings. The stage direction at his entrance is impressive: 'Jupiter descends in thunder and lighting, sitting upon an eagle'. Jupiter personifies the theme that humankind depends on providence for well-being.

Justice

Marginal character in *Measure For Measure* (1604), who is a magistrate.

K

Katharine of Aragon, Queen of England (1485-1536)

A major character in *Henry VIII* (1613), Katharine was the first of Henry's numerous wives. This play, by Shakespeare and Fletcher, was known as *All Is True* in their day, and is indeed quite accurate as to the facts. Katharine, a Spanish princess, has been Henry's wife for about 20 years and is presented as a mature character, but still beautiful and of such a rare personality that the sympathy of the auditor is entirely with her, and not with her adversaries, Henry and Cardinal Wolsey. The great

eighteenth-century actress Sarah Siddons, and the polymath Dr Samuel Johnson both felt Katharine was the greatest female character in the works of Shakespeare.

The play focuses on the King's desire to divorce Katharine, and marry Anne Boleyn. The reason he gives is that Katharine was his brother's widow, and hence his long-standing marriage to her is now on his conscience; he is also, however, desperate for a male heir. Katharine is required to face a divorce trial, but refuses to recognise the jurisdiction of the court. She does, however, address the assembly in an eloquent defence of her marriage and her long loyalty. This lengthy speech begins:

Sir, I desire you do me right and justice,
And to bestow your pity on me; for
I am a most poor woman, and a stranger,
Born out of your dominions, having here
No judge indifferent, nor no more assurance
Of equal friendship and proceeding. Alas, sir,
In what have I offended you? . . .

She then rounds on Cardinal Wolsey, her stern enemy, and addresses him with equal eloquence, but eventually he brings about the Queen's downfall. In an earlier scene, this exemplary woman has spoken to the King on the people's behalf against unjust taxes introduced by Wolsey. For this and other reasons, he wants to get rid of her. The King's lust does the rest, and he marries Anne. Katharine is retired from court with the title Princess Dowager. In her last scene, we see her near death; she falls asleep and has a dream of heavenly reward. This is an on-stage masque which is, unhappily, usually omitted from modern productions.

Henry VIII has considerable pageantry, and was particularly popular on eighteenth- and nineteenth-century stages, when heavy scenery was in vogue. Undoubtedly the greatest interpreter was Sarah Siddons, who kept Queen Katharine in her repertoire for nearly a quarter of a century, acting with several of her brothers. Her niece, Fanny Kemble, also took the role of Queen Katharine. In the nineteenth century, Ellen Terry acted Katharine opposite Irving in London, but she also appeared for her one and only performance at Stratford-on-Avon in this character in 1903, to mark Shakespeare's birthday. In modern times, Dame Peggy Ashcroft with the Royal Shakespeare Company, and Claire Bloom on the BBC, have acted Queen Katharine with great distinction.

Katherina

The heroine of *The Taming of the Shrew* (*c*.1594), Katherina is the elder of two daughters of Baptista, a gentleman of Padua. Katherina is wildly volatile, and her temper is famous far and near; she is clearly very unhappy, but her shrewish temperament makes it unlikely she will find a husband, and Baptista will not let her sister Bianca marry first. However, a fortune-hunter, one Petruchio, comes to town and, tempted initially by Katherina's dowry, undertakes to tame her. As the play is a farce, his manner of doing this is rough, and there is a great deal of knock-about courtship both before and after the marriage. This seeming mis-alliance does lead to genuine love between the two at the end, but the manner of Katherina's subjection can be distasteful to modern audiences. In her very lengthy speech at the end, addressing a banquet with two other wives present, Katherina gives a long exposition of the role of the dutiful wife. To the modern auditor, this speech seems rather demeaning, and is certainly more enjoyable cast in the form of a song in the musical, *Kiss Me, Kate* (1948), by Cole Porter, based on the play.

Fie, fie, unknit that threat'ning, unkind brow,
And dart not scornful glances from those eyes
To wound thy lord, thy king, thy governor. . . .
I am ashamed that women are so simple
To offer war where they should kneel for
    peace,
Or seek for rule, supremacy, and sway
When they are bound to serve, love, and obey.

Katherine

Lady-in-waiting to the Princess of France in *Love's Labour's Lost* (*c*.1598).

Katherine, Princess, later Queen of England
(1401-38).

The French Princess Katherine is a small character, but the leading woman, in the

Elizabeth Taylor as Katherina and Richard Burton as Petruchio in Zeffirelli's 1967 film.

Jenny Quayle as Princess Katherine with Michael Pennington as Henry V, 1987.

chronicle play, *Henry V* (*c*.1599). Her two scenes in the play are delicious gems. In the first, she has a humorous English lesson with Alice, her lady-in-waiting. In the second, she is wooed by the victorious young English King in his halting French. She has a sweet but rather sketchy character, and most of her dialogue is in French or broken English.

Keeper
Characters known as 'keepers' appear in *Henry VI Parts 1 and 3* (*c*.1592/*c*.1595); *Richard II* (*c*.1597); *Richard III* (*c*.1597); and *Henry VIII* (1613). These roles are minor male functionaries.

Kent, Earl of
An important secondary character in *King Lear* (1608), this nobleman remains faithful to the aged King in all his calamities. Early in the story Kent is banished for his blunt loyalty, and goes into disguise, which enables him to keep trying to help the King. Kent witnesses the old King's death, but it is implied that he will not long survive his master.

Kings
Eight visions appear in one scene of *Macbeth* (1606), representing future kings of Scotland.

Knight(s)
Walk-on male figures designated as 'knights' appear in *King Lear* (1608), *Pericles, Prince of Tyre* (*c*.1609), and *The Two Noble Kinsmen* (*c*.1613).

L

Lady
Characters known as 'lady' appear in *Richard II* (*c*.1597), *Timon of Athens* (*c*.1604), *Cymbeline* (1611), and *The Winter's Tale* (1611).

Laertes
This earnest and impetuous young man is an important secondary character in *Hamlet* (*c*.1602). Initially Laertes is a friend of the hero, but when Hamlet accidentally kills his father, Polonius, and indirectly causes the madness and death of his sister Ophelia, Laertes becomes the Prince's deadly enemy. As both Laertes and Hamlet are seeking revenge for their father's deaths, they are to a degree contrasted characters, but Laertes stoops to more unscrupulous means. However, it is significant that in the final death scene he and Hamlet exchange forgiveness. Laertes is young and lacks judgement.

Lafew, Lord
This marginal character in *All's Well That Ends Well* (*c*.1603), is an elderly friend of the Countess of Rossillion.

Lamprius
A walk-on male attendant in *Antony and Cleopatra* (1608).

Lancaster, John of Gaunt, Duke of
See Gaunt.

Lancaster, Prince John of
See Bedford.

Geoffrey Hutchings as Launce with Heidi as Crab, 1981.

Lartius, Titus

Legendary character in *Coriolanus* (1608), a Roman general of marginal importance.

Launce

This comic servant of Proteus, one of *The Two Gentlemen of Verona* (*c*.1598), takes on an importance out of all proportion to the size of his role. This is because he is the owner of Crab, the dog, one of the playwright's brilliant strokes of fancy. In two hilarious scenes with the dog, Launce speaks two monologues concerning his pet. No matter what the dog does during these speeches, the scenes are invariably a sensation in the theatre.

Laurence, Friar

An important secondary character in *Romeo and Juliet* (*c*.1597), this elderly clergyman is the well-meaning friend of the hero and performs the secret marriage of the lovers. Although a very careful reading of the text might find the morality of the Friar somewhat suspect and his actions a bit cowardly, in performance this largely passes unnoticed and we take him as benign. He is the counterpart of Juliet's Nurse, in so far as each are confidants of the two lovers and her advice is likewise less than wise.

Lavache

Court jester to the elderly Countess of Rossillion in *All's Well That Ends Well* (*c*.1603).

Lavinia

This distressed heroine is an important character in the revenge tragedy *Titus Andronicus* (*c*.1594) and is the daughter of the title character. She is raped by two brothers, who then cut out her tongue and cut off her hands to prevent her from informing against them. Although the story is repulsive in the extreme, Peter Brook produced an extremely well-received production for the Royal Shakespeare Company, starring Laurence Olivier and with Vivien Leigh as Lavinia, in what must rank as the best performance of this semi-mute female character.

Lawyer

A walk-on part in *Henry VI Part I* (*c*.1592).

Le Beau

A very minor character in *As You Like It* (1600).

Lear, King

The title character in the play which some consider the summit of Shakespeare's achievement, *King Lear* (1608). Lear is an ancient, probably mythical, King of Britain. He is 80 years old, and senility might be the best explanation of his

ABOVE Leonie Mellinger as Lavinia, 1981.
BELOW Edwin Forrest as King Lear, 1887.

Richard Briers as Lear with Emma Thompson as the Fool, 1990.

You Heavens, give me that patience, patience
  I need!–
You see me here, you Gods, a poor old man,
As full of grief as age; wretched in both!
If it be you that stirs these daughters' hearts
Against their father, fool me not so much
To bear it tamely; touch me with noble anger,
And let not women's weapons, water-drops,
Stain my man's cheeks! No, you unnatural
  hags,
I will have such revenges on you both
That all the world shall – I will do such things,
What they are yet I know not, but they shall
  be
The terrors of the earth. You think I'll weep;
No, I'll not weep:
I have full cause of weeping, but this heart
Shall break into a hundred thousand flaws
Or ere I'll weep. O Fool! I shall go mad.

This speech is punctuated by the first
stage direction referring to the coming
storm, which occupies the long central
section of the play and also parallels the
gathering storm in Lear's mind, vestiges
of which can already be noted in the
above speech. As his daughters' cruelty
exposes the poor old man to wander the
heath in the storm, his arrogance is seen
to greatly decrease and his awareness of
the sufferings of others increases.

Poor naked wretches, wereso'er you are,
That bide the pelting of this pitiless storm,
How shall your houseless heads and unfed
  sides,
Your loop'd and window'd raggedness, defend
  you
From seasons such as these? O! I have ta'en
Too little care of this. Take physic, Pomp;
Expose thyself to feel what wretches feel,
That thou mayst shake the superflux to them,
And show the Heavens more just.

The bleak death of the innocent Cordelia
has been much remarked, and indeed in
the notorious version of the play by
Nahum Tate, the ending was revised to
let her live. But Shakespeare does allow
the tender reconciliation of the father and
daughter, before their deaths in Act V.
The final entry of the King with the dead
Cordelia in his arms is one of the most
tragic moments in the canon, and his
extended eulogy for her very beautiful.

Howl, howl, howl! O! you are men of stones:

behaviour, which is irrational much of the
time. Yet Lear meets the classical
requirements of the tragic hero, in that he
does achieve a considerable degree of self-
awareness by the end of the tragedy, and
is far more sensitive to the sufferings of
others.

When we first meet Lear, he is acting
as the all-powerful monarch, but his
action is to abdicate and divide his
kingdom amongst his three daughters. In
addition to arrogance, he also displays
lack of awareness of the true natures of
his offspring, Regan, Goneril and
Cordelia. He rewards the hypocritical and
evil daughters, but banishes Cordelia for
her blunt honesty and failure to flatter
him. Gradually the King learns the
difference, and addresses the two elder
daughters:

Had I your tongues and eyes, I'd use them so
That heaven's vault should crack. She's gone
  for ever. . .

Lear was first acted by Richard Burbage, but scholars think the play was not well received in Shakespeare's day or soon after. Certainly the purity of the text has received short shrift until modern times. In 1681 Nahum Tate wrote his adaptation, in which the happy ending was only one of the travesties. His text was used in part or in whole by Thomas Betterton, David Garrick (Lear being his greatest role), John Philip Kemble, Edmund Kean and Edwin Booth. In 1838, William Charles Macready introduced a more accurate text, but even so eminent an actor as Henry Irving cut more than half of the play, and was a failure in it. Great modern interpreters have included John Gielgud and Paul Scofield at Stratford, in 1950 and 1962 respectively.

Robert Stephens plays Lear, 1993.

The darker moods of the play, its outright cruelties, and the seeming agnosticism have fallen on more responsive ears in the modern era. It has been filmed many times, but two media productions in particular must be cited. Laurence Olivier's award-winning television performance, his last role in Shakespeare, brought the play to larger audiences in Britain and America than the stage could do. More recently, the BBC radio production to mark the 90th birthday of Sir John Gielgud (1994) consolidated his position as one of the all-time great Lears. The advanced age of both Olivier and Gielgud did not admit of strenuous stage performances, but that very factor added a poignancy to characterisations on television and radio.

Legate
A bit part in *Henry VI Part I* (*c*.1592), a minor male functionary of the Pope.

Lennox, Thane of
A bit part in *Macbeth* (1606), a Scottish noble.

Leonardo
A servant in *The Merchant of Venice* (*c*.1598).

Leonato
An important secondary character in *Much Ado About Nothing* (*c*.1599), Leonato is the Governor of Messina where the action takes place. He is the kindly father and uncle respectively of the two heroines, Hero and Beatrice.

Leonine
A minor figure in *Pericles, Prince of Tyre* (*c*.1609) who is hired to murder the heroine, Marina.

Leontes
A leading character in *The Winter's Tale* (1611), Leontes is King of Sicilia and the irrationally jealous husband of Hermione. Convinced that his Queen has committed adultery with the visiting King of Bohemia, he brings her to trial and

condemns the Queen's newborn daughter to be abandoned in the wilderness. His mania darkens the first half of the play, but the second takes place 16 years later, by which time his daughter, Perdita, has grown up as a charming shepherdess. Leontes finally learns wisdom after he applies to the oracle of Apollo at Delphi, which confirms Hermione's innocence. It takes divine intervention to change his opinion, as his under-developed character is chiefly delineated by his obsession.

Lepidus, Marcus Aemilius

A minor but important historical character in *Julius Caesar* (1599) and *Antony and Cleopatra* (1608), Lepidus is shown as a bit of a dolt. He is the third member, with Mark Antony and Octavius Caesar, of the triumvirate which rules Rome after the assassination of Julius Caesar. The ease with which his partners dominate him adds to the political background of the two plays.

Lewis XI, King of France (1423-1483)

Historical character in *Henry VI Part 3* (*c*.1595), whose role is secondary.

Lieutenant

Several male walk-ons in *Henry VI Parts 2 and 3* (*c*.1594/*c*.1595) and *Coriolanus* (1608).

Ligarius, Caius (Quintus)

A minor historical character in *Julius Caesar* (1599), one of the assassins.

Lincoln, Bishop of

Historical character who is the confessor of *Henry VIII* (1613).

Litio

The name Hortensio takes when he disguises himself as a music teacher in *The Taming of the Shrew* (*c*.1594).

Lodovico

Minor character in *Othello* (1604), who appears near the end as a messenger from Cyprus.

Johnston Forbes-Robertson as Leontes.

Lodowick

The name the Duke takes when he goes into disguise in *Measure for Measure* (1604).

Longaville

One of three young lords attending on the King of Navarre in *Love's Labour's Lost* (*c*.1598), who agree to his plan to take a vow giving up romance and revels in favour of study for a set period of time. Like the others, however, he falls in love.

Bernard Wright as Longaville with Simon Russell Beale as the King of Navarre, 1990.

Lord(s)

A lord, or lords, are called for in the following plays: *The Taming of the Shrew* (c.1594); *King John* (c.1595); *Richard II* (c.1597); *Love's Labour's Lost* (c.1598); *Henry IV Part 1* (1598); *Much Ado About Nothing* (c.1599); *As You Like It* (1600); *Hamlet* (c.1602); *All's Well That Ends Well* (c.1603); *Macbeth* (1606); *Coriolanus* (1608); *Timon of Athens* (c.1604); *Pericles, Prince of Tyre* (c.1609); *Cymbeline* (1611); and *The Winter's Tale* (1611).

Lorenzo

Secondary character in *The Merchant of Venice* (c.1598), one of the three young swains of Venice who fall in love with the three women in the story. Lorenzo elopes with Jessica, Shylock's daughter, and thus is party to a Jewish-Christian marriage which is important to the plot. He is a stylish aristocrat, but with little substance.

Lovell, Sir Francis

Minor historical character in *Richard III* (c.1597), an unsavoury supporter of the title character.

Lovell, Sir Thomas

Minor historical character in *Henry VIII* (1613), who is a supporter of Cardinal Wolsey and subsequently of Bishop Gardiner.

Lucentio

The successful suitor to Bianca in the sub-plot of *The Taming of the Shrew* (c.1594), Lucentio is depicted as a stereotyped young lover.

Lucetta

A minor figure, maid to Julia in *The Two Gentlemen of Verona* (c.1598).

Luciana

A lively young woman who is the secondary heroine in *The Comedy of Errors* (c.1594), and sister to Adriana.

RIGHT Francesca Annis as Luciana, with Roger Rees as Antipholus of Syracuse, 1976.

Lucianus

A minor character who appears in the play-within-a-play in *Hamlet* (c.1602), entitled 'The Murder of Gonzago'. When not enacting this playlet, he is merely known as Player.

Lucilius

Minor historical figure in *Julius Caesar* (1599), who is an officer in Brutus' army.

Lucilius

A servant in *Timon of Athens* (c.1604).

Lucio

A marginal figure in *Measure For Measure* (1604), who is a somewhat unpleasant friend of the condemned Claudio. Lucio is a customer in the bordello, and is shown as generally dissolute.

Lucius

A secondary character who is a son to the title character in *Titus Andronicus* (c.1594).

Lucius

A young servant of Brutus in *Julius Caesar* (1599).

Lucius

An Athenian aristocrat, who proves an ungrateful friend to the title character in *Timon of Athens* (c.1604).

Lucius

A secondary character in *Cymbeline* (1611), Lucius first appears as an envoy to the British King from Rome. Later he commands the Roman army and employs the disguised heroine, Imogen, as his page. Lucius is a noble soldier.

Lucius' Servant

A minor character who is an attendant of Lucius in *Timon of Athens* (c.1604).

Lucullus

Ungrateful friend of Timon in *Timon of Athens* (c.1604), and also an Athenian aristocrat.

Lucy, Sir William

A minor officer in *Henry VI Part 1* (c.1592).

Lychorida

A minor character in *Pericles, Prince of Tyre* (c.1609), who is the nurse of the heroine, Marina.

Lysander

This young man is an important character in *A Midsummer Night's Dream* (1598), one of the two sets of lovers who get lost in the enchanted woods and are subjected to the tricks of Puck, the fairy. Lysander

Dick Powell as Lysander and Olivia de Havilland as Hermia in Reinhardt's film.

loves Hermia, but Puck's machinations transfer his love temporarily to Helena, with hilarious results. The two young men, Demetrius and Lysander, are less fully delineated than are the two girls, so casting is important to correct this.

Lysimachus
A secondary character in *Pericles, Prince of Tyre* (*c*.1609), Governor of Mytilene in this romance. He visits the trapped Marina, daughter of Pericles, in a brothel, but recognising her virtue, spares her. Pericles later bestows Marina on Lysimachus. His is a stereotyped character, an aristocrat of sufficient discretion to marry the heroine.

M

Macbeth
The title character in *Macbeth* (1606), Shakespeare's shortest tragedy, is a Scottish nobleman. He is a brave military leader, but he murders his King and kinsman, and usurps his throne. Shakespeare took material from Holinshed's *Chronicles* concerning the reigns of the real Kings Duncan and Macbeth (1034-57 AD), but his tragedy is more concerned with the individual versus the powers of hell. Macbeth is specifically seen in the context of supernatural forces. The three witches, who open the play in a prologue-like scene, personify these powers of hell. The theme is damnation, and no amount of directorial interference in a modern production can get away from that. Damnation requires the acquiescence of the person damned. Both Macbeth and Banquo, as comrades-in-arms, are tempted by the witches' prophecies, but Banquo does not succumb to their seduction. Macbeth has a moral choice, and he self-destructs. His character is introspective, at first indecisive, and self-absorbed; he is highly intelligent and has considerable powers of imagination. These are all qualities of the tragic hero, whose function is to achieve self-

John Gielgud plays Macbeth, 1942.

awareness in the course of the action. In the first of his great soliloquies Macbeth says:

If it were done when 'tis done, then 'twere
     well
It were done quickly. If the assassination
Could trammel up the consequence, and catch
With his surcease success – that but this blow
Might be the be-all and the end-all here,
But here, upon this bank and shoal of time,
We'd jump the life to come. But in these cases
We still have judgement here – that we but
     teach
Bloody instructions, which, being taught,
     return
To plague the inventor. . . .
                              Besides, this Duncan
Hath borne his faculties so meek, hath been
So clear in his great office, that his virtues
Will plead like angels, trumpet-tongued
     against
The deep damnation of his taking-off; . . .

Macbeth knows that the price of his ambition is his own 'deep damnation', and it takes the ruthless spur of his wife, Lady Macbeth, to focus his decision to

Orson Welles directed and starred in the film of *Macbeth*, 1948.

murder Duncan. In the earlier part of the play she seems stronger than her husband, but once they have achieved the crown, this is reversed. Macbeth is aware of the evil which his 'vaulting ambition' will cause, but he refuses to resist temptation. At the end of the daggers scene Macbeth says:

To know my deed, 'twere best not know
  myself.
Wake Duncan with thy knocking. I would
  thou couldst!

Yet he sinks further into sin with the murder of Banquo and the attempted murder of his young son, Fleance, who escapes. He then puts to the sword the wife and children of Macduff, and by the end of the play Macbeth has become isolated and de-humanised. Yet his self-awareness grows, and he suffers and despairs over his wickedness, rather than gloating in it. He recognises the good in himself which has been wasted:

I have lived long enough: my way of life
Is fallen into the sere, the yellow leaf;
And that which should accompany old age,
As honour, love, obedience, troops of friends,
I must not look to have . . .

His high intelligence, personal bravery and love for his wife are stressed by the author to the bitter end. It is the announcement of her death which triggers Macbeth's famous meditation on the futility of life.

She should have died hereafter.
There would have been a time for such a
  word –
Tomorrow, and tomorrow, and tomorrow,
Creeps in this petty pace from day to day
To the last syllable of recorded time:
And all our yesterdays have lighted fools
The way to dusty death. Out, out, brief
  candle!
Life's but a walking shadow, a poor player
That struts and frets his hour upon the stage
And then is heard no more. It is a tale
told by an idiot, full of sound and fury,
Signifying nothing.

The sense of a wasted life which this speech, and the play as a whole, engenders in the auditor is reinforced by the emphasis laid on Macbeth's bravery and intelligence in the final moments of the play. Yet it is right and satisfying that Macbeth is killed (offstage) by Macduff,

David Garrick plays Macbeth.

who thus avenges the murder of his innocent family.

Like Hamlet, the role of Macbeth has attracted all the great actors, but not a few poor performances have been chalked up along the way. It is presumed that the immensely versatile Richard Burbage was the first Macbeth. After the Restoration and in the early eighteenth century, Thomas Betterton and James Quin acted notable Macbeths in adapted versions. David Garrick restored some, but not all, integrity to the text, and made Macbeth one of his best characterisations. Charles Macklin was well-dressed for the part, introducing plaids and kilts. John Philip Kemble, as was his wont with tragedy, acted a very slow Macbeth. In the nineteenth century, two American stars, Edwin Booth and Edwin Forrest, were excellent as Macbeth, but the latter developed an unfortunate rivalry on both sides of the Atlantic with William Charles Macready, especially where *Macbeth* was concerned. Henry Irving was also a fine Macbeth. In 1941, New York enjoyed an especially noteworthy production directed by Margaret Webster, which starred Maurice Evans and was filmed some 20 years later. In London, Michael Redgrave, John Gielgud and Laurence Olivier all played the part. One of the best productions of recent years was Trevor Nunn's for the Royal Shakespeare Company, for which he staged a studio version in rehearsal clothes and bare stage, and with no interval. His stars, Ian McKellen and Judi Dench, were superb and this was later televised.

Macbeth, Lady

As wife of the title character in *Macbeth* (1606), this Scottish noblewoman shares his lust for power, and also shares his confidence. In her very first entry she is reading a letter from him in which he confides to her the witches' prophecies, referring to her as 'my dearest partner of greatness'. In a lengthy soliloquy, Lady Macbeth invokes the powers of darkness in one of Shakespeare's greatest speeches for a female character.

Sarah Siddons, the greatest Lady Macbeth, 1783.

> . . . . Come, you spirits
> That tend on mortal thoughts, unsex me here
> And fill me from the crown to the toe top-full
> Of direst cruelty. Make thick my blood;
> Stop up the access and passage to remorse,
> That no compunctious visitings of nature
> Shake my fell purpose, nor keep pace between
> The effect and it. Come to my woman's
>   breasts
> And take my milk for gall, you murdering
>   ministers,
> Wherever, in your sightless substances,
> You wait on nature's mischief. Come, thick
>   night,
> And pall thee in the dunnest smoke of hell,
> That my keen knife see not the wound it
>   makes,
> Nor heaven peep through the blanket of the
>   dark
> To cry, 'Hold, hold!'

In her character, as in her husband's, we see the acceptance of damnation as the price for achieving her desired ambition, the crown. On arrival at their castle, Macbeth's first words to his wife are 'My dearest love'. The love between the two is nowadays seen as sexually intense, at least in the early scenes. When he hesitates in carrying out the murder, she uses her sexuality to steel him to his task by implying that failure to carry out the crime which will make her Queen indicates he does not love her, and she further stings him with an accusation of effeminacy. Lady Macbeth refers to her son, a carryover from Shakespeare's sources, although no such child appears in the play. Macbeth, having been convinced to act, says:

> Bring forth men-children only!
> For thy undaunted mettle should compose
> Nothing but males.

It will be seen that within the first act of the play are the seeds for two possible interpretations of Lady Macbeth. Either she is a ferocious and perversely brave woman who fears not even hell itself, one who is as ruthlessly ambitious as her husband is, or she has a softer, more feminine side to her nature. The latter traits are consistent with her mental breakdown and ultimate suicide, as the weight of her crime overwhelms her. Perhaps the real challenge for the actress is to indicate both components in this complex character. Her viciousness in the early scenes weakens considerably once the Macbeths have achieved the crown. Macbeth's intimacy with his wife also declines, and she is not a party to his later crimes. In her sleepwalking scene, however, she does indicate an awareness that Lady Macduff has been murdered, and that the death of Banquo weighs heavily on her husband. Her sleepwalking scene, unlike her great soliloquy invoking evil spirits in Act I, is written in short, disjointed sentences, which are punctuated by the comments of the doctor and waiting woman who are watching her. The contrast in the first and final appearance of Lady Macbeth is marked by the switch from poetry to prose, and by her complete reversal from strength to utter collapse. 'Hell is murky', she says in her final scene. Deranged though she now is, Lady Macbeth recognises her bleak fate. The final speech of the play is spoken by Malcolm, the new King. He refers to the Macbeths as:

This dead butcher and his fiend-like queen–
Who, as 'tis thought, by self and violent hands
Took off her life –

Frances Tomelty as Lady Macbeth in the sleepwalking scene, 1980

For centuries, Lady Macbeth has been considered Shakespeare's supreme achievement in female characterisation, although Cleopatra would run her a close second in modern opinion. In the early part of the eighteenth century the greatest Lady Macbeth was Hannah Pritchard, who acted the role for 20 years. Later in the century, Sarah Siddons, who acted the character for 25 years, was universally acclaimed. She is still considered the greatest exponent; her 'Notes on the Character of Lady Macbeth' indicate her awareness of the dual nature of the character. It was the great nineteenth-century French actress, Sarah Bernhardt, however, who was the first to bring out the overt sexuality of the character, which has become so much a feature of twentieth-century interpretations. American actresses of the nineteenth century who excelled in the part include Charlotte Cushman and Helena Modjeska. Ellen Terry followed the softer approach to the character when first acting it. Modern performances which have been highly regarded include Dame Sybil Thorndike, Dame Judith Anderson, and Dame Judi Dench.

Judi Dench as Lady Macbeth with Ian McKellen as Macbeth, 1976.

Macduff, Thane of Fife
Probably a historical figure, Macduff is an important character in *Macbeth* (1606). After Macbeth ascends the throne of Scotland, Macduff joins Malcolm, the son of the murdered King Duncan, in England, where he and Malcolm attempt to raise the means to fight the tyrant. Macduff is a brave and virtuous Scottish nobleman. When he learns that the usurper has put his wife and children to the sword, he is incited to personal vengeance, and he is the one to kill Macbeth. Macduff, rather than either of the two sons of the late Duncan, is the agent of divine retribution on the evil Macbeth.

Macduff, Lady
This young mother has a small but very vital role in *Macbeth* (1606); she has only one scene, that in which she and her children are murdered. 'Children' should be emphasised, as some productions show her only with her young boy, aged about ten. The text stresses several times that she has more than one child, and so a baby should be in her arms when she is apprehended. Obviously, a baby in addition to the boy greatly adds to the guilt of Macbeth.

Macmorris, Captain
An Irish officer in the army of *Henry V* (*c*.1599). Macmorris appears only in the emblematic scene where an Irish, Scottish, English and Welsh soldier come together, with somewhat comic effect.

Maecenas, Caius
Historical figure who is a follower of Octavius Caesar in *Antony and Cleopatra* (1608).

Magnificoes of Venice
Silent male figures who serve as legal officials to the Duke of Venice in the trial scene of *The Merchant of Venice* (*c*.1598).

Malcolm
A secondary character in *Macbeth* (1606), Malcolm is the elder of King Duncan's two sons and is designated his heir. The

character of Malcolm is noble and brave, but not particularly fully developed. As the new King, he speaks the closing passage of the play.

Malvolio

An important character in *Twelfth Night* (1602), Malvolio is a middle-aged, puritanical steward to the Countess Olivia. He is extremely pompous, but nevertheless the trick which Sir Toby Belch and his cohorts play on Malvolio is carried to cruel extremes, when the steward is not only thoroughly humiliated but also imprisoned. The central episode of *Twelfth Night* is the gulling of Malvolio, and this is such an outstandingly funny scene that leading actors from Thomas Betterton to Laurence Olivier have always been willing to take the role.

ABOVE Ellen Terry as Mamillius, in her first stage appearance, with Charles Kean as Leontes, 1856.
LEFT Donald Wolfit as Malvolio, 1940.

Mamillius

A little boy in *The Winter's Tale* (1611), Mamillius is the pert young son of King Leontes and Queen Hermione. He dies of grief due to his father's mistreatment of the Queen.

Man

Walk-ons who are simply designated 'man' are needed in *Richard II* (*c*.1597); *Troilus and Cressida* (*c*.1603); and *Henry VIII* (1613).

Marcade

A messenger in *Love's Labour's Lost* (*c*.1598).

Marcellus

A minor character in *Hamlet* (*c*.1602), who is one of the sentries on the ramparts. Marcellus speaks the famous comment, 'Something is rotten in the state of Denmark', which is a theme of the play.

Marcus Andronicus

A secondary character in *Titus Andronicus* (*c*.1594), brother of the title character.

Mardian

This eunuch is an attendant on the Queen of Egypt in *Antony and Cleopatra* (1608).

Margarelon

A legendary and minor character in *Troilus and Cressida* (*c*.1603), the bastard son of King Priam of Troy.

Margaret of Anjou, later Queen of England (1430-82)

A character of major importance in the works of Shakespeare, as she appears in the whole of his trilogy of *Henry VI Parts 1, 2 and 3* (*c*.1592/*c*.1594/*c*.1595) and in *Richard III* (*c*.1597). Taking the whole sweep of her character, which is very long in stage time, she is unquestionably one of the author's greatest female characterisations. Only the relative unfamiliarity of the trilogy prevents a better appreciation of Shakespeare's achievement with this character. Margaret was the niece of King Charles VII of France, but was considered of rather inferior status to marry the young King Henry VI. Her character develops from a young and somewhat green girl, who arrives as a prisoner of Suffolk who has convinced the English King to marry her, to a warrior Queen and central figure in the Wars of the Roses, and finally to a raging old hag crying vengeance on her enemies.

It is suggested that she becomes the lover of Suffolk; certainly she is mismatched with the introspective, pious Henry. Gradually she completely dominates him, and even goes into battle in his place. It is interesting that the trilogy shows two women warriors, Joan of Arc and Margaret of Anjou, both Frenchwomen. Margaret's cruel nature is seen at its worst in Part 3, when she taunts her enemy, Richard, Duke of York, with his pretensions to the crown. She and her followers put a paper crown upon their prisoner's head, and she wipes his face with a napkin stained with his young son's blood.

Brave warriors, Clifford and Northumberland,
Come, make him stand upon this molehill
   here,
That wrought at mountains with outstretched
   arms
Yet parted but the shadow with his hand.
(To York) What – was it you that would be
   England's king?
Was't you that revelled in our Parliament,
And made a preachment of your high descent?
Where are your mess of sons to back you now?
The wanton Edward and the lusty George?
And where's that valiant crookback prodigy,
Dickie, your boy, that with his grumbling
   voice
Was wont to cheer his dad in mutinies?
Or with the rest where is your darling
   Rutland?
Look, York, I stained this napkin with the
   blood
That valiant Clifford with his rapier's point
Made issue from the bosom of thy boy.
And if thine eyes can water for his death,
I give thee this to dry thy cheeks withal.

Her speech continues and when York can get a word in edgewise, he addresses her in the famous phrase, 'She-wolf of France, but worse than wolves of France. . . . O tiger's heart wrapped in a woman's hide!' The latter line was parodied by Robert Greene, the Elizabethan playwright, in the earliest written reference to Shakespeare. Queen Margaret is ambitious and brave, but utterly unscrupulous. Yet she has her sufferings, such as when, in her final defeat at the Battle of Tewkesbury, she is forced to witness the murder of her son, the Prince of Wales.

Genevieve Ward as Queen Margaret.

In *Richard III* she is depicted as an aged and decrepit fury, who rages around the edges of the action in the first half of the play. Her role is smaller in that play, and her most effective moment is the so-called 'weeping queens' scene in which Queen Margaret, Queen Elizabeth and the old Duchess of Gloucester bemoan their fates in an emblematic, choral episode outside the Tower of London. In stagings which include the four plays as part of a season, the role of Margaret is a great unifying force, as she is the only character who appears in all four. Dame Peggy Ashcroft gave a memorable reading of the role with the Royal Shakespeare Company some years back.

Margaret

At attendant on the lesser of the two heroines, Hero, in *Much Ado About Nothing* (c.1599).

Maria

A secondary character in *Love's Labour's Lost* (c.1598), she is a lady-in-waiting to the Princess of France and falls in love with Longaville.

Maria

An important comic character in *Twelfth Night* (1602), Maria is the chambermaid to the Countess Olivia, and conspires with Sir Toby, Sir Andrew, and Feste to play a trick on Malvolio, the Countess' pompous steward. The 'gulling of Malvolio' into thinking the Countess loves him is the central action of the play. Maria is lively and clever, and at the end marries Sir Toby, her employer's uncle.

Mariana

A minor character in *All's Well That Ends Well* (c.1603).

Mariana

A minor character in *Measure For Measure* (1604), Mariana is nevertheless important for the resolution of the plot. By means of a 'bed trick' Mariana replaces the heroine, Isabella, in the bed of the would-be seducer, Angelo. As Mariana is the former love of Angelo, she gets her revenge on him and he is required by the Duke to marry her.

Marina

Daughter of the title character in *Pericles, Prince of Tyre* (c.1609). Although Marina is only present in the last two acts, hers is an important character and is beautifully

ABOVE Athene Leyler as Maria, with Roger Liverly as Sir Toby Belch, Moreland Graham as Feste and Richard Goolder as Sir Andrew Aguecheek, 1933.
BELOW Felicity Dean as Marina, with Gerard Murphy as Pericles, 1983.

written. In arguments about what part of the play Shakespeare wrote, and who might be his unknown collaborator, it is always claimed for him that he wrote Marina. She is a spirited, virtuous young woman who triumphs in the face of incredible adversities in this very episodic tale. Her name reflects her birth at sea and, like Perdita in *The Winter's Tale* (1611), Marina is an infant in the beginning who is separated from her parents.

Mariner
Minor character who appears in *The Winter's Tale* (1611) and *The Tempest* (1611).

Marshall, Lord
A very minor functionary in *Richard II* (*c*.1597).

Marshall
A very minor official at the court of Simonides in *Pericles, Prince of Tyre* (*c*.1609).

Martext, Sir Oliver
A country clergyman in *As You Like It* (1600), whose name indicates his character.

Martius
Minor character in *Titus Andronicus* (*c*.1594), a son of the title character.

Martius
The name by which *Coriolanus* (1608) is known until he receives the title 'Coriolanus'.

Marullus
A small, historical character in *Julius Caesar* (1599), a supporter of Brutus and a tribune.

Masquers
A small group of non-speaking revellers in *Romeo and Juliet* (1597).

Master
Walk-ons of a nautical nature needed in *Henry VI Part 2* (*c*.1594) and *The Tempest* (1611).

Master-Gunner
Minor French soldier in *Henry VI Part 1* (*c*.1592).

Mate
A walk-on sailor in *Henry VI Part 2* (*c*.1594).

Mayor of Coventry
Minor figure in *Henry VI Part 3* (*c*.1595).

Mayor of London
Minor figure in *Henry VI Part 1* (*c*.1592), *Richard III* (*c*.1597) and *Henry VIII* (1613).

Mayor of St Albans
Minor figure in *Henry VI Part 2* (*c*.1594).

Mayor of York
Minor figure in *Henry VI Part 3* (*c*.1595).

Melun, Giles de, Lord
Marginal historical character in *King John* (*c*.1595).

Menas
Marginal historical figure in *Antony and Cleopatra* (1608), he is a pirate and a follower of Pompey.

Menecrates
Marginal historical figure in *Antony and Cleopatra* (1608), also a pirate and follower of Pompey.

Menelaus
A legendary character and minor figure in *Troilus and Cressida* (*c*.1603), Menelaus is the hapless husband of the captive Helen of Troy and one of the Greek commanders at Troy.

Menenius Agrippa
A legendary figure and important secondary character in *Coriolanus* (1608), the elderly, loyal friend of the title figure. The character of Menenius is delineated by his political wisdom.

Menteith, Thane of
A marginal historical character in *Macbeth* (1606), one of the Scottish thanes fighting the title character.

Merchant
Walk-on characters required in *The Comedy of Errors* (*c*.1594) and *Timon of Athens* (1604).

Mercutio
An important secondary character in *Romeo and Juliet* (1597), Mercutio is a friend of the hero who is slain by Tybalt,

thus contributing to Romeo's banishment, since he in turn kills Tybalt. Mercutio speaks the celebrated comic monologue beginning 'O, then I see Queen Mab hath been with you'. This very long, and nearly incomprehensible, speech was given its best recent rendering by Michael Kitchen in a Royal Shakespeare Company production.

Michael Kitchen as Mercutio with Sean Bean as Romeo, 1987.

Messala, Marcus Valerius
Minor historical character in *Julius Caesar* (1599), a military subordinate of Brutus and Cassius.

Messenger
One or more messengers are required in *Henry VI Part 1* (*c*.1592); *Henry VI Part 2* (*c*.1594); *The Comedy of Errors* (*c*.1594); *Titus Andronicus* (*c*.1594); *King John* (*c*.1595); *Richard III* (*c*.1597); *The Merchant of Venice* (*c*.1598); *Henry IV Part 1* (1598); *Henry V* (1599); *Much Ado About Nothing* (*c*.1599); *Julius Caesar* (*c*.1599); *Henry IV Part 2* (1600); *Hamlet* (*c*.1602); *All's Well That Ends Well* (*c*.1603); *Measure For Measure* (1604); *Othello* (1604); *Timon of Athens* (*c*.1604); *Macbeth* (1606); *Antony and Cleopatra* (1608); *Coriolanus* (1608); *Pericles, Prince of Tyre* (*c*.1609); *Cymbeline* (1611); *Henry VIII* (1613) and *The Two Noble Kinsmen* (*c*.1613).

Metellus Cimber
A minor historical character in *Julius Caesar* (*c*.1599), one of Caesar's assassins.

Michael
Follower of Jack Cade in *Henry VI Part 2* (*c*.1594).

Michael, Sir
Follower of the Archbishop of York in *Henry IV Part 1* (1598).

Milan, Duke of

The father of the heroine, Silvia, in *The Two Gentlemen of Verona* (*c*.1598). He is the ruling authority, but his role is relatively minor.

Miranda

This very young lady is the heroine of *The Tempest* (1611), the author's last play written alone. She has been exiled with her father Prospero, a magician, to an enchanted island. Miranda is fourteen, but unlike the character of Juliet at that age, Miranda is nothing like as demanding on the actress. She does not speak much, but displays compassion and imagination. Her most famous line is:

How beauteous mankind is! O brave new
   world,
That has such people in 't!

Miranda falls in love with Ferdinand, who has been shipwrecked on the island.

Zena Walker as Miranda and Alexander Davion as Ferdinand, 1952.

Montague

Father of the hero in *Romeo and Juliet* (1597), Montague is less important than the father of Juliet, but both are mature men of stubborn character. They are Veronese noblemen.

Montague, Lady

A very minor character in *Romeo and Juliet* (1597), she is the mother of Romeo. She speaks only one line, and has died of grief before the final scene in the lovers' tomb.

Montague, John Neville, Lord

A minor historical character in *Henry VI Part 3* (*c*.1595).

Montano

A minor character in *Othello* (1604), he is the Governor of Cyprus.

Montgomery, Sir John

A marginal historical figure who is a supporter of Edward IV in *Henry VI Part 3* (*c*.1595).

Montjoy
A minor character in *Henry V* (*c.*1599), a French herald who has a number of telling exchanges with the English King.

Mopsa
A very minor role, a shepherdess in *The Winter's Tale* (1611).

Morgan
The name taken by the banished courtier, Belarius, in *Cymbeline* (1611).

Morocco, Prince of
Minor figure in *The Merchant of Venice* (*c.*1598), his role is nevertheless important as one of the three suitors to the heroine, Portia. He must choose between the three mysterious caskets of gold, silver and lead. His choice, gold, is wrong. Morocco is one of the few black characters in the author's work.

Mortimer, Lady Catherine
A small role in *Henry IV Part 1* (1598), this historical figure speaks only Welsh

ABOVE Hepburn Graham as the Prince of Morocco, 1984.
BELOW *The Death of Mortimer*, from *Henry VI*, after a painting by James Northcote.

and must converse with her husband through her father's translating. Though this obviously causes a casting problem, it is a pity to drop her dialogue as its adds colour. She also sings a song in Welsh.

Mortimer, Sir Edmund, Earl of March
Historical figure found in *Henry VI Part 1* (*c.*1592), uncle of the claimant to the throne, Richard of York.

Mortimer, Edmund, Earl of March
Historical figure found in *Henry IV Part 1* (1598), who is a rebel against Henry.

Mortimer, Sir Hugh
Bit part in *Henry VI Part 3* (*c.*1595), a Yorkist and uncle of Richard, Duke of York.

Mortimer, Sir John
Minor historical figure in *Henry VI Part 3* (*c.*1595), a Yorkist supporter and brother of the above.

Morton
A rebel against Henry IV in *Henry IV Part 2* (1600).

Morton, John, Bishop of Ely
Historical but minor figure in *Richard III* (*c*.1597), a pawn of Richard's.

Moth
A fairy in *A Midsummer Night's Dream* (1598) who is an attendant on Titania. Moth can be of either sex, but should be small and agile.

Moth
A page in *Love's Labour's Lost* (*c*.1598) who attends Armado.

Mouldy, Ralph
A rustic in *Henry IV Part 2* (1600), one of the very funny recruits who fall victim to Sir John Falstaff's conscriptions for the King's army; upon offering a bribe, Mouldy is released.

Mowbray, Thomas, Duke of Norfolk
A secondary character in *Richard II* (*c*. 1597), an enemy of Bolingbroke, the future King.

Mowbray, Thomas, Lord
Marginal historical figure in *Henry IV Part 2*, (1600), one of the rebels against the King and the son of the Mowbray in *Richard II*.

Murderers
Bit parts in *Henry VI Part 2* (*c*.1594), *Richard II* (1597) and *Richard III* (*c*.1597).

Musicians
The plays of Shakespeare are very musical, and this includes not only specific songs with words, but non-verbal music as well. We find musicians in *The Two Gentlemen of Verona* (*c*.1598); *The Merchant of Venice* (*c*.1598); *Romeo and Juliet* (1597); *Much Ado About Nothing* (*c*.1599); *Henry IV Part 2* (1600); *Twelfth Night* (1602); *Othello* (1604); and *Cymbeline* (1611).

The Fairies, less than graceful in *A Midsummer Night's Dream*, 1989.

Mustardseed
A fairy in *A Midsummer Night's Dream* (1598), who is an attendant on Titania. Like Moth, Mustardseed could be either sex, but is usually small and agile.

Mutius
Minor character in *Titus Andronicus* (*c*.1594), a son of the title character, who is killed by his father.

Myrmidon
Several minor characters in *Troilus and Cressida* (*c*.1603) who, according to classical mythology, were followers of Achilles. He is a major character, and he orders the Myrmidons to kill Hector, the Trojan Prince. This they do on finding him without his armour, a dishonourable act.

Mytilenian Sailor
Also known as 'Tyrian', a walk-on in *Pericles, Prince of Tyre* (*c*.1609).

N

Nathanial
Minor figure who is a comic curate and companion of Holofernes in *Love's Labour's Lost* (*c.*1598).

Nathanial
A very minor member of Petruchio's zany household in *The Taming of the Shrew* (*c.*1594).

Neighbour
Any one of three supernumeraries in *Henry VI Part 2* (*c.*1594).

Nell
A kitchenmaid in the household of Adriana, in *The Comedy of Errors* (*c.*1594). Nell is a very small role; much of her dialogue is shouted from offstage.

Nell
A walk-on part, a country wench in *The Two Noble Kinsmen* (*c.*1613) who, with four other girls, performs a dance.

Nerissa
Important secondary character in *The Merchant of Venice* (*c.*1598). Nerissa is not a servant; she is the live-in companion of the heroine, Portia. She joins her mistress in travelling to Venice where they both appear disguised as a lawyer and a lawyer's clerk in the trial of Shylock. Nerissa therefore, is a 'breeches part'. She is a pert, lively and attractive young woman who forms part of the three marriage couples at the end of the comedy.

Josette Simon as Nerissa, 1984.

Nestor

A legendary figure, an old man in *Troilus and Cressida* (*c*.1603), who is one of the Greek leaders beseiging Troy.

Nicanor

Minor character in *Coriolanus* (1608), a traitor to Rome.

Nicholas

Like Nathanial, he is a comic servant in the household of Petruchio in *The Taming of the Shrew* (*c*.1594).

Nobleman

A supernumerary in *Henry VI Part 3* (*c*.1595).

Norfolk, John Howard, Duke of

A minor historical character in *Richard III* (*c*.1597), he commands the army of King Richard at Bosworth Field, the battle which concludes the play.

Norfolk, Thomas Howard, Duke of

A courtier of the King in *Henry VIII* (1613), Norfolk is an enemy of Cardinal Wolsey.

Norfolk, John Mowbray, Duke of

A minor follower of the Yorks in *Henry VI Part 3* (*c*.1595).

Norfolk, Thomas Mowbray, Duke of

A secondary historical figure in *Richard II* (*c*.1597), who is an enemy of Bolingbroke, the future King.

Northumberland, Henry Percy, Earl of

This historical character is found in *Richard II* (*c*.1597), and *Henry IV Parts 1 and 2* (1598/1600). In *Richard II* he supports Henry Bolingbroke, but he rebels against him as King Henry. He is not a congenial personality and is less important in the later plays, although he is the father of Hotspur.

Northumberland, Henry Percy, Earl of

Minor historical character, found in *Henry VI Part 3* (*c*.1595) as a supporter of the pious King.

Northumberland, Lady

Historical character in *Henry IV Part 2* (1600), she is an older woman whose part is quite small. She is the wife of the Earl of Northumberland and mother of Hotspur.

Nurse

A minor non-speaking character in *Henry VI Part 3* (*c*.1594).

Nurse

A minor non-speaking character in *Titus Andronicus* (*c*.1594), murdered by Aaron to keep her silent.

Nurse

A major comic character, the Nurse is the friend and confidante of the heroine in *Romeo and Juliet* (1597). Although the Nurse lives in the very cosmopolitan city of Verona, she is very like many rustic characters in the author's work. She is hearty, bawdy and very loving to Juliet, although her advice is poor; verbosity is one of her chief characteristics.

Mrs. Stirling as Juliet's Nurse, 1882.

Nym

A dim follower of Sir John Falstaff, Nym is an eccentric character found in *The Merry Wives of Windsor* (*c*.1597) and *Henry V* (*c*.1599).

Nymphs

Female dancers in *The Tempest* (1611), who perform with the reapers.

O

Oatcake, Hugh

A small comic part in *Much Ado About Nothing* (*c*.1599), Hugh Oatcake is one of the night watch with Dogberry.

Oberon

The Fairy King in *A Midsummer Night's Dream* (1598) is one of the author's most lyrical characters. Oberon has quarrelled with his wife Titania, the Queen of the Fairies.

Oberon
Ill met by moonlight, proud Titania.
Titania
What, jealous Oberon. Fairies, skip hence;
I have forsworn his bed and company.

Oberon decides to play a trick on her and, while he is about it, to help the four young mortal lovers who are lost in the enchanted woods. He sends his servant, Puck, to fetch a magic flower:

Jean Forbes-Robertson plays Oberon, 1933.

I know a bank where the wild thyme blows,
Where oxlips and the nodding violet grows,
Quite over-canopied with luscious woodbine,
With sweet musk-roses, and with eglantine.
There sleeps Titania sometime of the night,
Lull'd in these flowers with dances and
    delight;
And there the snake throws her enamell'd
    skin,
Weed wide enough to wrap a fairy in;
And with the juice of this I'll streak her eyes,
And make her full of hateful fantasies.

Oberon is gentle and kind to the four young lovers, and eventually lifts his mischievous spell from Titania. Oberon and Titania, re-united, bless the royal marriage of Duke Theseus and Hippolyta, the Queen of the Amazons, with which the comedy concludes. The *Dream* has always been popular in one form or another, but prior to the twentieth century was the subject of severe alterations. In 1914, Harley Granville-Barker staged an avant-garde production which, while controversial, paid strict attention to the correct text. In 1937, an Old Vic production gave the ballet dancer Robert Helpmann his first theatrical role, as Oberon. In 1970, in the famous Peter Brook production for the Royal Shakespeare Company, Alan Howard doubled as Theseus and Oberon.

LEFT Sylvia Shaw as Octavia, 1935.

Octavia

Historical character who is of secondary importance in *Antony and Cleopatra* (1608). 'Admir'd Octavia' is the sister of Octavius Caesar and becomes the new wife of the widowed Mark Antony. Although much loved by her brother, she is a political pawn to cement the partnership of Caesar and Antony. The marriage has the opposite effect, however, when Antony goes back to his mistress, Cleopatra. Octavia is shown as a respectable Roman widow, who tries to tread the difficult path of loyalty to her new husband and her brother. We only meet her in three scenes, but her actions and demeanour are in every way admirable and sympathetic. 'Gentle Octavia', Antony calls her, and this contrasts her very strongly with Cleopatra, which is the principal purpose of her character. Neither of the two women are young in the context of the play. When Cleopatra asks her spy to guess at Octavia's years and is informed that her rival is about thirty, it is clear from the Queen's response that she does not at all like this answer, as she herself is older.

Officer(s)

One or more officers are needed in *Henry VI Part 1* (c.1592); *The Comedy of Errors* (c.1594); *The Taming of the Shrew* (c.1594); *Twelfth Night* (1602); *Othello* (1604); *King Lear* (1608); *Coriolanus* (1608); and *The Winter's Tale* (1611).

Old Athenian

A supernumerary in *Timon of Athens* (c.1604).

Old Lady

A very small role in *Henry VIII* (1613).

Old Man

Minor character found in *Macbeth* (1606) and *King Lear* (1608).

Oliver

A secondary character in *As You Like It* (1600), Oliver is the villainous older brother of Orlando, the hero. His reformation into a character sufficiently good to attract the sudden love of Celia at the end is scarcely believable, but as it comes about due to Orlando's saving his life, it passes scrutiny in the theatre.

Olivia

The Countess Olivia is one of the two heroines of *Twelfth Night* (1602). She has inherited an estate but has no immediate family and wears mourning dress for her dead brother. She is an independent young woman who is used to managing her own affairs and she rejects the suit of her neighbour, Count Orsino, who is in love with her. Olivia is somewhat over-emotional, veering from excessive mourning and a retreat from life, to an over-zealous passion for an unknown young man who has appeared at her gate, and who is actually Viola in disguise as a young man. Olivia's extremes never quite come under control, as she abruptly transfers her passion to Viola's twin brother, Sebastian, in the closing scenes, yet her elegance and high intelligence make her an appealing heroine.

Ophelia

A beautiful young noblewoman at the
Danish court, who is the love of the title
character in *Hamlet* (*c*.1602). She is one of
a family of three who are closely allied to
the royal family of three. Both her father,
Polonius, and her brother, Laertes, have
cautioned her against believing in Prince
Hamlet's love, as they feel that her rank
may not be high enough to aspire to be
the Prince's bride. That Hamlet
genuinely loves her, or did love her
before he became obsessed with his
mother's hasty remarriage, is made quite
clear. Ophelia is a gentle, loving creature
but she is not mentally strong; her
subsequent rejection by Hamlet, and his
accidental killing of her father, push her
over the brink into madness. Her so-
called 'mad scene' is almost impossibly
difficult for the modern actress, but it is
touching and heartbreaking to read. It is
also interesting for the symbolic use

ABOVE Mrs Patrick Campbell as Ophelia.
BELOW Sara Crowe as Olivia with Eric Porter
as Malvolio, Maria Miles as Viola and
David Ryall as Feste, 1991.

which Shakespeare makes of flowers, and this feature has made Ophelia a frequent subject of painters. The poor insane girl sings as she distributes her flowers to the King, the Queen, and her brother.

Ophelia
There's rosemary, that's for remembrance; pray you, love, remember. And there is pansies, that's for thoughts.
Laertes
A document in madness: thoughts and remembrance fitted.
Ophelia
There's fennel for you, and columbines. There's rue for you. And here's some for me. We may call it herb of grace a Sundays. O, you must wear your rue with a difference. There's a daisy. I would give you some violets, but they withered all when my father died. They say a made a good end. (sings) For bonny sweet Robin is all my joy.

A question mark hangs over Ophelia's death. Was it suicide, or accidental? The evidence in the play is conflicting, and possibly Shakespeare meant to leave it ambiguous. The ritual of her funeral is given considerable prominence.

Orlando

Earnest young hero of *As You Like It* (1600), who surprises the court in the first act of the play by defeating a very intimidating wrestler, Charles. As a result, Rosalind, the play's principal heroine, falls instantly in love with Orlando. Both have reason to flee the court, and are destined to meet in the Forest of Arden. Orlando performs a number of noble acts in the forest, such as his tender care for his aged servant, Adam, and his saving of his wicked brother's life (offstage). Our real interest is in seeing the maturing of his love for Rosalind, but his character is not fully developed and he is definitely upstaged by the resourceful Rosalind.

Orleans, Charles, Duke of

Historical character in *Henry V* (c.1599), who is of secondary importance. He is one of the rather arrogant French officers who meet King Henry at Agincourt.

Jack Hawkins as Orsino with Anna Neagle as Olivia, 1934.

Orsino, Duke

Romantic leading man in *Twelfth Night* (1602), who is the passionately sentimental suitor of his neighbour, Countess Olivia, but she does not return his love. Orsino is moody and self-obsessed; the famous speech with which he opens the play makes it clear that he is in love with love:

If music be the food of love, play on,
Give me excess of it that, surfeiting,
The appetite may sicken and so die.
That strain again, it had a dying fall.
O, it came o'er my ear like the sweet sound
That breathes upon a bank of violets,
Stealing and giving odour. Enough, no more,
'Tis not so sweet now as it was before.
O spirit of love, how quick and fresh art thou
That, notwithstanding thy capacity
Receiveth as the sea, naught enters there,
Of what validity and pitch so e'er,
But falls into abatement and low price
Even in a minute! So full of shapes is fancy
That it alone is high fantastical.

He becomes attached to his new page, Cesario, who is really Viola disguised as a youth. This provides the happy ending since, when her womanhood is revealed,

Orsino quickly transfers his love from Olivia to Viola. The issue of gender is a bit ambiguous in *Twelfth Night*.

Osric

A minor character in *Hamlet* (*c*.1602), Osric is what in later English drama became known as a fop; a courtier at the Danish court, he is a comic dandy.

Ostler

A small role in *Henry IV Part 1* (1598), a groom.

Oswald

The steward of one of the King's wicked daughters in *King Lear* (1608), Oswald acts on her instructions to behave insolently to the aged King. His pomposity degenerates into villainy, and he is finally killed off by the virtuous Edgar.

Othello

The title character in one of the author's greatest tragedies, *Othello* (1604), he is also a rare instance in the plays of a black character. Othello is a man of mature years, a general in the Venetian army. He knows little of life outside his military career, certainly nothing of women, and he is an alien outsider in the sophisticated city of Venice. He is a noble figure who claims to be of royal blood; his deadly enemy, Iago, refers to Othello's 'free and open nature', and his 'constant, loving, noble nature'. Othello is initially a devout Christian, but as his obsessional jealousy of his new wife, Desdemona, takes hold of him, he reverts to paganism in his speech and mental attitudes. This aspect of his character emphasises how incomplete is his integration into Venetian society; he is a mercenary soldier whose superb skills have put him in a position of command in an alien society.

It is significant, however, that only Iago, Othello's mortal enemy, and Brabantio, his new father-in-law, express any colour prejudice, and the latter is understandably distraught at the defection of his daughter. The full title of the play, *The Tragedy of Othello, the Moor of Venice*, is only one of numerous references to him as a Moor. Shakespeare's decision to depict a black man as his tragic hero was unusual and courageous; blackamoors in earlier plays were associated with evil and death. Aaron in *Titus Andronicus* (*c*.1594) follows this tradition, while Shakespeare's only other black character, the Prince of Morocco in *The Merchant of Venice* (*c*.1598), is made to look ridiculous. In *Othello*, however, we are closer to the idea of 'the noble savage' who is destroyed by his corrupting connection with the white man's society. The story *Othello* is not essentially original, as Shakespeare uses a tale by Giambattista Cinzio Giraldi, published in 1565, but what he does with his material is sublimely his own. The alleged infidelity of Desdemona is so improbable, and hangs on such flimsy

Paul Robeson as Othello, 1950.

Ben Kingsley plays Othello, 1986.

evidence, that a man of Othello's intelligence would hardly credit it, were it not for the difference in their race and age, and his lack of knowledge of women of her class. *Othello* is a domestic tragedy whose violent climax hinges on the hero's tragic flaw of jealousy, and on the depth of his passion for his new wife.

When Othello first arrives through a storm to take command of Cyprus, he greets his wife, who arrives separately, with exquisite expression.

It gives me wonder great as my content,
To see you here before me. O, my soul's joy!
If after every tempest come such calms,
May the winds blow till they have wakened
    death,
And let the labouring bark climb hills of seas,
Olympus-high, and duck again as low
As hell's from heaven. If it were now to die,
'Twere now to be most happy; for I fear
My soul hath her content so absolute
That not another comfort like to this
Succeeds in unknown fate.

Unhappily, his foreboding proves all too true. Near the end, Othello contemplates his sleeping wife with love, but his obsessional jealousy is so strong that he murders her with deliberation.

It is the cause, it is the cause, my soul:
Let me not name it to you, you chaste stars!
It is the cause. Yet I'll not shed her blood,
Nor scar that whiter skin of hers than snow,
And smooth as monumental alabaster:

Yet she must die, else she'll betray more men.
Put out the light, and then put out the light:
If I quench thee, thou flaming minister,
I can again thy former light restore,
Should I repent me; but once put out thy
    light,
Thou cunning'st pattern of excelling nature,
I know not where is that Promethean heat
That can thy light relume. When I have
    plucked thy rose,
I cannot give it vital growth again,
It needs must wither. I'll smell it on the
    tree.
(He kisses her).

Othello's powers of expression are one of his most marked features, and greatly enhance his dignity and sympathy as a character. His suicide scene, once he recognises his fault, is heartbreaking, especially in a strong stage performance. His sense of loss, and his acceptance of damnation for his act, is brave and absolute.

Who can control his fate? 'Tis not so now.
Be not afraid, though you do see me
    weaponed:
Here is my journey's end, here is my butt
And very sea-mark of my utmost sail.
Do you go back dismayed? 'Tis a lost fear:

Willard White as Othello with Imogen Stubbs as Desdemona, 1989.

Man but a rush against Othello's breast,
And he retires. Where should Othello go?
Now, how dost thou look now? O ill-starred
wench,
Pale as thy smock! When we shall meet at
compt
This look of thine will hurl my soul from
heaven
And fiends will snatch at it. Cold, cold, my
girl,
Even like thy chastity.
O cursed, cursed slave! Whip me, ye devils,
From the possession of this heavenly sight!
Blow me about in winds! Roast me in sulphur!
Wash me in steep-down gulfs of liquid fire!
O Desdemon! Dead Desdemon! Dead! O! O!

The redoubtable Richard Burbage
created the part in Shakespeare's lifetime.
In the nineteenth century, Edmund Kean
was the greatest Othello, and some
historians would still give him the palm.
The first great black Shakespearean, Ira
Aldridge (c.1807-1867) was noted for the
role. It is also interesting, given the
musicality of Othello's dialogue and the
extreme demands which the role places
on the actor's speech, that two singers,
Paul Robeson and Willard White, have
achieved critical success in the role. The
former played it in London in 1930, but
not until 1942 was it possible for him,
under the direction of Margaret Webster,
to tour the USA and play *Othello* on
Broadway, for almost 300 performances.
This was then a record for an American
Shakespearean production. Robeson
again acted the role in 1950, this time
with the Royal Shakespeare Company in
England. Willard White, the opera star,
has had recent success in a studio
production with the Royal Shakespeare
Company, which was also televised.
Although white actors, such as Laurence
Olivier with the National Theatre, have
continued to distinguish the role, this is
increasingly unacceptable to audiences.
An RSC production of recent years fell
back on the old idea that a Moor was
actually an Arab-related racial type, and
in that context Ben Kingsley gave an
excellent performance.

RIGHT Constance Collier as Anne Page, c.1906.

Outlaws
Minor characters in *The Two Gentlemen of
Verona* (c.1594).

Overdone, Mistress
A minor character in *Measure For Measure*
(1604), who is the keeper of a brothel.

Oxford, John de Vere, Earl of
Historical figure who is found in *Henry
VI Part 3* (c.1595) and *Richard III*
(c.1597); his role is marginal.

P

Page (s)
One or more pages are called for in *The
Taming of the Shrew* (c.1594); *Richard III*
(c.1597); *Romeo and Juliet* (1597); *Henry
IV Part 2* (1600), *As You Like It* (1600);
All's Well That Ends Well (c.1603); *Timon
of Athens* (c.1604); and *Henry VIII* (1613).

Page, Anne
The courtship of Anne Page by three
suitors forms the subplot in *The Merry
Wives of Windsor* (c.1597). She is the
pretty young daughter of one of the
'merry wives' whose gulling of Sir John
Falstaff forms the main plot.

Page, George
This middle-aged man in *The Merry Wives
of Windsor* (c.1597) is the father of Anne
Page and her younger brother, William.

Mr Page is the husband of one of the 'merry wives', Mrs Margaret Page; he is easy-going, and a pleasant example of small-town life. The play is characterised by the realistic rendering of village characters, of which Page is one. His role is not as large as the other husband, Mr Ford.

Page, Mrs Margaret

A prosperous townswoman in *The Merry Wives of Windsor* (*c*.1597); she and her friend Mrs Ford are the title characters. Both ladies receive identical love letters from the fat knight, Sir John Falstaff, and they resolve to get even with him for his presumption. As they are both witty and resourceful, Sir John is really no match for them. Mrs Page is given a fuller context with respect to her family, as she is the mother of Anne Page (of marriageable age) and William Page (a typical schoolboy). Mrs Page is also seen giving a dinner party in the first act, to which most of the important characters are invited. *Merry Wives* is Shakespeare's only contemporary play, set not only in his own time, but with a wealth of realistic detail, no doubt observed from his home-town, Stratford, rather than Windsor. The companionable relationship of the two lively wives is one of the joys of this farce.

Page, Master William

This young lad is a character in *The Merry Wives of Windsor* (*c*.1597), whose small role takes on an importance out of proportion to its size since it is probably a portrait of Shakespeare himself as a child of ten or eleven years. Master William is put through his paces in the scene known as 'the Latin lesson', when his Welsh schoolmaster calls on the boy to recite for the benefit of his anxious mother. The text used is the one Shakespeare would have used as a pupil at the Stratford Grammar School, where it is known that he likewise had a Welsh schoolmaster. Young William Page's scene is a delightful vignette, and he figures in a minor way elsewhere in the farce.

Painter

A minor character in *Timon of Athens* (*c*.1604) who, together with a Poet, hope to exploit the generosity of the lead character by presenting him with examples of their works.

Palamon

One of the title characters in *The Two Noble Kinsmen* (*c*.1613) by Shakespeare and John Fletcher. Palamon and Arcite are two knights whose friendship is first jeopardised and then destroyed when they fall in love with the same lady while they are both imprisoned at Athens. In this play the characterisation is weak. It was produced by the Old Vic in 1928, and by the Shakespeare Festival in Regent's Park in the 1970s.

Pandar

Minor character in *Pericles, Prince of Tyre* (*c*.1609) who, with his wife, keeps the bordello where the heroine, Marina, is imprisoned.

LEFT Janet Dale as Mrs Page with Lindsey Duncan as Mrs Ford, 1985.

Paris

A legendary prince of Troy in *Troilus and Cressida* (*c*.1603). A dissolute young man, he has, before the play opens, stolen Helen from her husband, Menelaus, causing the Trojan War. Paris is the brother of Troilus and Hector, all of whom are sons of King Priam.

Parolles

A follower of Bertram, the anti-hero in *All's Well That Ends Well* (*c*.1603), he is a '*miles gloriosus*' stock figure from Roman comedy, a blustering, braggart soldier, of whom there are several in Shakespeare's plays. Parolles is a coward who pretends to be a warrior and nobleman.

Patience

A walk-on who is a lady-in-waiting to Queen Katharine in *Henry VIII* (1613).

Pandarus

A legendary character in *Troilus and Cressida* (*c*.1603), Pandarus is the uncle of the unfaithful heroine, Cressida. Although a comic figure, Pandarus is as cynical as his symbolic name would suggest. He is part of the corrupt and bitter world of this long play.

Pandulph

Historical figure of marginal importance in *King John* (*c*.1595). A papal legate, he is an enemy of the title character.

Panthino

A minor character in *The Two Gentlemen of Verona* (*c*.1598), who is a servant.

Paris

This young knight is a suitor to the heroine in *Romeo and Juliet* (1597), and is to be forced upon her by her parents' wishes. He is a stereotyped young lover and contrasts dismally with Romeo, who kills Paris in Juliet's tomb, not even realizing who his victim is.

Queen Katharine of Aragon with Patience, after the painting by C.R. Leslie.

Patroclus

A legendary character in *Troilus and Cressida* (*c*.1603), a Greek warrior and follower of Achilles, whose death induces Achilles to resume fighting.

Paulina

This energetic lady of mature years is a highlight of *The Winter's Tale* (1611). Although a friend and confidante of Queen Hermione, the character of Paulina is so well-rounded as to go well beyond the stereotype of a confidante. Paulina is forthright in her defence of the hapless Queen, falsely accused of adultery, and roundly denounces King Leontes for his injustice to his wife. Paulina contrives a way to save the condemned Queen and hide her away for 16 years, until the King comes to his senses and the baby he has renounced has grown up. She is an overbearing but loving woman, on whom the plot turns.

Elizabeth Spriggs as Paulina, with the infant Perdita, 1970.

Peaseblossom

One of the fanciful little fairies who attend on Titania in *A Midsummer Night's Dream* (1598).

Pendant

A marginal male character in *The Taming of the Shrew* (*c*.1594).

Pembroke, William Marshall, Earl of

A silent figure in *Henry VI Part 3* (*c*.1595), who is a supporter of Edward IV. Pembroke was an actual person.

Pembroke, William Marshall, Earl of

A minor historical character in *King John* (*c*.1595), an enemy of the King.

Penker, Friar

A minor historical figure, a corrupt clergyman in *Richard III* (*c*.1597).

Percy

See Hotspur, Henry Percy.

Percy

See Northumberland, Earl of.

Percy, Lady

This young woman, a historical character, has a small part in *Henry IV Parts 1 and 2* (1598/1600). Although her husband Hotspur (Henry Percy) calls her 'Kate', her name was Elizabeth; she was the daughter of Edmund Mortimer, Earl of March.

Perdita

A charming young heroine in *The Winter's Tale* (1611) who, having been abandoned as an infant in the first half of the play, is raised as a shepherdess, but later turns out to be the long-lost daughter of King Leontes and Queen Hermione of Sicilia. As she is actually a princess, she proves to be a suitable consort for Prince Florizel, the son of the former friend of Leontes, who has fallen in love with her. Perdita is similar in character to Ophelia before tragedy blighted her life. Both girls are associated with the symbolism of flowers, but Perdita in a much lighter vein. She

LEFT Judi Dench as Perdita, 1970; she doubled the role of Hermione.

Peter

A very minor character in *Henry VI Part 2* (*c*.1594) who is an apprentice to Thomas Horner, an armourer.

Peter

Marginal character in *Romeo and Juliet* (1597) who is a comic attendant on the Nurse; Peter was portrayed by Will Kempe in Shakespeare's company.

Peter

Minor character in *The Taming of The Shrew* (*c*.1594), a servant of Petruchio.

Peter of Pomfret

A minor historical figure in *King John* (*c*.1595).

Petitioners

Several supernumeraries who appeal to the court in *Henry VI Part 2* (*c*.1594).

Peto

A small part in *Henry IV Parts 1 and 2* (1598/1600), he is one of the eccentric drinking companions of Sir John Falstaff.

Douglas Hodge plays Pericles, 1994.

presents flowers to the father of Prince Florizel, King Polixenes, and his elderly aide, Camillo, who are in disguise.

For you there's rosemary and rue; these keep
Seeming and savour all the winter long;
Grace and remembrance be to you both,
And welcome to our shearing . . .
        Here's flowers for you:
Hot lavender, mints, savory, marjoram;
The marigold, that goes to bed with the sun
And with him rises weeping; these are flowers
Of middle summer, and I think they are given
To men of middle age. Y'are very welcome.

Pericles

The leading character in Shakespeare's late romance, *Pericles, Prince of Tyre* (*c*.1609), on which he seems to have had an unknown collaborator. Pericles is the ruler of Tyre, and is presented as a sort of 'everyman' figure who follows many paths and endures much suffering. He ages considerably in the course of the very episodic story, from a young man seeking love to a man of mature years who is the father of Marina, the heroine. The character of Pericles is one-sided and mainly virtuous; he passively accepts what fate sends him.

Petruchio

The leading male character in *The Taming of The Shrew* (*c*.1594), Petruchio is a young fortune-hunter in search of a wealthy wife. His character is not very congenial to modern tastes, as he is seen as the male chauvinist *par excellence*, who tames his new wife, Katherine, by unduly aggressive and humiliating behaviour towards her. The play is a farce, however, and the nature of farce is exaggeration. He may also somewhat exaggerate his military experience.

Have I not heard great ordnance in the field,
And heaven's artillery thunder in the skies?
Have I not in a pitched battle heard
Loud 'larums, neighing steeds, and trumpets'
    clang?
And do you tell me of a woman's tongue,
That gives not half so great a blow to hear
As will a chestnut in a farmer's fire?
Tush, tush – fear boys with bugs.

His bravado, of course, is combined with cunning in his manner of dealing with Katherina's shrewishness, and her attractiveness of person clearly has some positive first effect on Petruchio. In his

ABOVE Douglas Fairbanks as Petruchio with Mary Pickford in the 1929 film.
ABOVE RIGHT Timothy Dalton and Vanessa Redgrave in the *Shrew*, 1986.

first encounter with Katherina, he is not specifically depicted as striking her, although she strikes him, but stage practice usually incorporates spanking or some other mildly violent behaviour on his part. At their wedding, his manners are marked by his insultingly bizarre outfit, his very rude behaviour to her family and guests, and a threatening speech which says in part:

I will be master of what is mine own.
She is my goods, my chattels. She is my
    house,
My household-stuff, my field, my barn,
My horse, my ox, my ass, my anything,
And here she stands, touch her whoever dare.

On arrival at Petruchio's house, he starves his bride, prevents her from sleeping, and cunningly deprives her of new clothes while appearing to entertain the tailor. Later, on their way to visit her

father, Petruchio continues to infuriate Katherina with his madcap behaviour, until for the sake of peace she agrees with him. Much of the time Petruchio is role-playing in order to subdue Katherina, and that can be extended by a modern director to infer that Petruchio is really falling in love with Katherina and is a more subtle and likeable character than he at first appears.

Phebe

A delightful but small role, a shepherdess in *As You Like It* (1600). A haughty girl, who spurns the love of Silvius, she is taught a lesson about love by the heroine, Rosalind, and finally accepts Silvius.

Philario

A minor character in *Cymbeline* (1611), who is the host of the hero, Posthumus, and figures in the story of the wager on the virtue of his wife, Imogen.

Philemon

A minor servant in *Pericles, Prince of Tyre* (*c.*1609).

Philip

A small role of a servant in the hero's household in *The Taming of the Shrew* (*c.*1594).

Philip Augustus, King of France

Historical figure who is a supporter of the young claimant to the English throne, Prince Arthur, and an enemy of the title character in *King John* (*c.*1595). Philip is a devious character, but disappears from the play halfway through.

Philo

Minor character in *Antony and Cleopatra* (1608), who is one of the title character's soldiers. He makes the opening speech of the play, which summarises the situation and the relationship between the two lovers.

Nay, but this dotage of our General's
O'erflows the measure. Those his goodly eyes,
That o'er the files and musters of the war
Have glowed like plated Mars, now bend, now turn
The office and devotion of their view
Upon a tawny front. His captain's heart,

Which in the scuffles of great fights hath burst
The buckles on his breast, reneges all temper,
And is become the bellows and the fan
To cool a gipsy's lust.
   (Flourish. Enter Antony, Cleopatra, her
   ladies, the train, with eunuchs fanning her.)
Take but good note, and you shall see in him
The triple pillar of the world transformed
Into a strumpet's fool. Behold and see.

Philostrate

A minor functionary of the court of Duke
Theseus in *A Midsummer Night's Dream*
(1598), Philostrate is a mature man whose
office is that of Master of the Revels.

Philotus

Minor character in *Timon of Athens*
(*c*.1604), a servant.

Phrynia and Timandra

Minor characters who are concubines of
Alcibiades in *Timon of Athens* (*c*.1604).
They normally speak in unison and have
only the most superficial characters,
consistent with their calling, but their
greed in accepting gold from Timon is
stressed.

Pinch, Dr

A small stereotyped character, a 'quack
doctor', in *The Comedy of Errors* (*c*.1594).

Pindarus

A minor historical character in *Julius
Caesar* (1599) who, as the slave of one of
the conspirators, Cassius, assists his
master to commit suicide.

Pirates

Three walk-ons in *Pericles, Prince of Tyre*
(*c*.1609) who capture the heroine, Marina,
and sell her to a bordello.

Pirithous

Minor character in *The Two Noble
Kinsmen* (*c*.1613), who is a friend and
attendant of Duke Theseus.

Pisanio

Marginal character in *Cymbeline* (1611), a
faithful servant of the hero, Posthumus,
and later of his wife, Imogen.

William Mollison as Pistol, 1905.

Pistol

Comic braggart soldier in *Henry IV Part 2*
(1600), *The Merry Wives of Windsor*
(*c*.1597), and *Henry V* (*c*.1599). Pistol is a
type drawn from Roman comedy, the
'*miles gloriosus*' figure of the proud soldier
whose grandiose behaviour wreaks havoc.
Pistol speaks in exaggerated language
which is probably intended as literary
parody, and although much of this is
hopelessly dated now, Pistol is so well
drawn that we enjoy him regardless; his
symbolic name announces a loud and
funny character. Pistol is a follower of Sir
John Falstaff. The character was given an
unforgettable performance by Robert
Newton in Olivier's film of *Henry V*.

Player King

Character in the play-within-the-play in
Hamlet (*c*.1602), which is known as *The
Murder of Gonzago*. The person enacting
the Player King is usually the First
Player.

Player Queen

Character in the play-within-the-play in
Hamlet (*c*.1602).

Players

A group of minor figures who participate in the induction scene which opens *The Taming of The Shrew* (c.1594).

Players

A group of touring players who are secondary characters in *Hamlet* (c.1602). They confer with Hamlet about the performance he wishes them to give before his uncle and the court.

Plebeians

Walk-ons who are important in *Julius Caesar* (1599) as the Roman citizens who respond to Mark Antony's impassioned speech and react to Caesar's assassination.

Poet

A minor and foolish character in *Julius Caesar* (1599).

Poet

A minor figure in *Timon of Athens* (c.1604) who, with a Painter, exploits the generosity of the title character.

Poins, Ned

A secondary character in *Henry IV Parts 1 and 2* (1598/1600), one of Prince Hal's drinking companions at the Boar's Head Tavern. Poins suggests the two tricks that the Prince plays on Sir John Falstaff, and is part of the low-life scene which the Prince must reject when he inherits the crown.

Polixenes, King of Bohemia

One of two kings in *The Winter's Tale* (1611) who are good friends in the beginning, but whose friendship is destroyed by the obsessive and unwarranted jealousy of Leontes, the King of Sicilia, who accuses his wife, Queen Hermione, of adultery with Polixenes. This bleak story is contrasted with events 16 years later, when the children of the two kings fall in love and finally marry. The character of Polixenes must therefore age considerably during the course of the play, but otherwise his bland personality develops little; he remains an elegant aristocrat in a fairy tale.

Polonius

This old man is an important secondary character in *Hamlet* (c.1602). He is a minister of the King of Denmark, and his two adult children, Laertes and Ophelia, live with Polonius at court when the former is not away following his fortunes. Polonius's advice to Laertes before his son's departure from court in the early part of the play is his most famous speech and ends:

This above all – to thine own self be true,
And it must follow, as the night the day,
Thou canst not then be false to any man.
Farewell – my blessing season this in thee.

Yet Polonius himself is devious and his love of spying and intrigue is his undoing. When he is eavesdropping on Hamlet's intense conversation with his mother, the Prince hears a noise behind the arras, or curtain, and stabs the old man. His death is a turning point in the play. There is considerable comedy in his character, as he is a bit stupid and long-winded, but it seems shocking that Hamlet feels so little remorse at his death.

Polydore

The name under which Guiderius, the King's son, is raised by an old hermit in *Cymbeline* (1611).

RIGHT Frank Middlemass as Polonius with Virginia McKenna as Gertrude, 1984.

Pompey

A marginal character in *Measure For Measure* (1604) who is a pimp in the bordello run by Mistress Overdone. He is a humorous, low-life figure.

Pompey (Sextus Pompeius)

Historical figure in *Antony and Cleopatra* (1608), who is a rebel against the triumvirate of Octavius, Mark Antony and Lepidus. Pompey's key moment is when he invites Antony, Caesar and others to a feast on board his galley by way of patching up their quarrels. This colourful scene adds atmosphere to the play, but Pompey then disappears from the action. He is the son of Pompey the Great, a major figure in history but who does not feature in this play.

Popilius Lena

Marginal historical figure in *Julius Caesar* (1599), a Roman senator.

Porter

A porter or gatekeeper is required in *Henry VI Part 1* (c.1592); *Henry IV Part 2* (1600); *Macbeth* (1606); and *Henry VIII* (1613). The Porter in *Macbeth*, although a small part, is of considerable importance as one of those Shakespearean clowns used for comic relief at a moment of high tragic tension. He is the gatekeeper at Macbeth's castle, and hears a knocking at the gate just after the Macbeths have completed the murder of King Duncan. In his drunkeness, the Porter pretends to be the gatekeeper of hell, which is appropriate as the Macbeths have just lost their souls in their act of dire murder. When the Porter opens the gate, he finds Macduff, who will, in the fullness of time, be the agent of vengeance on Macbeth. The Porter's comedy therefore has a more serious undertone.

Portia

The heroine of *The Merchant of Venice* (c.1598), Portia is one of the author's most pleasing creations. She is an independent young woman who has been left a fortune, but is constrained by her father's will to marry only the suitor who successfully de-codes the riddle of the three chests of gold, silver and lead. Her marriage to Bassanio, though happily achieved, is immediately put in peril by the consequences of her new husband's debts. His friend Antonio (the merchant) is in danger of forfeiting a pound of his flesh to the Jewish usurer, Shylock, in payment of an agreed bond. Up to this point Portia's character has conformed to conventional norms, although she is shown as wise beyond her years. She under-rates herself when giving her hand to Bassanio, in a celebrated speech.

You see me, Lord Bassanio, where I stand,
Such as I am. Though for myself alone
I would not be ambitious in my wish
To wish myself much better, yet for you
I would be trebled twenty times myself,
A thousand times more fair, ten thousand
   times more rich,
That only to stand high in your account
I might in virtues, beauties, livings, friends,
Exceed account. But the full sum of me
Is sum of something which, to term in gross,
Is an unlessoned girl, unschooled,
   unpractised,
Happy in this, she is not yet so old
But she may learn; happier than this,
She is not bred so dull but she can learn;
Happiest of all is that her gentle spirit
Commits itself to yours to be directed
As from her lord, her governor, her king.

Within the confines of her household, Portia has been fully in command, but her true resourcefulness now manifests itself in a public venue. Going into the Venetian court disguised as an eminent male lawyer, Portia devises the ingenious scheme by which Antonio's life is saved and Shylock defeated. But she first asks Shylock to show mercy, in a speech which is one of Shakespeare's great orations.

The quality of mercy is not strained.
It droppeth as the gentle rain from heaven
Upon the place beneath. It is twice blest:
It blesseth him that gives, and him that takes.
'Tis mightiest in the mightiest. It becomes
The throned monarch better than his crown.
His sceptre shows the force of temporal
    power,
The attribute to awe and majesty,
Wherein doth sit the dread and fear of kings;
But mercy is above this sceptred sway.
It is enthroned in the hearts of kings:
It is an attribute to God himself,
And earthly power doth then show likest
    God's
When mercy seasons justice . . .

Having failed in her appeal to Shylock, Portia then considers his bond and points out that he may take neither more nor less than a pound of flesh, and is not entitled to spill any blood.

Like a number of the heroines of the comedies, Portia is a 'breeches part'; only in that guise could she play so decisive a role in a man's world. The definitive interpreter of the part was Dame Ellen Terry, who acted Portia opposite Henry Irving's Shylock at the Lyceum for many years at the end of the nineteenth century, making her last appearance with him in 1903.

Portia

A small but significant role in *Julius Caesar* (1599), Portia is a historical figure and the wife of Brutus. In order to inspire her husband with the confidence to tell her of the impending plot against Caesar, Portia shows Brutus a self-inflicted wound in her thigh, demonstrating that she has the high Roman virtue of self-control. Later, when her husband's fortunes decline, we hear of her suicide. The nobility of Portia was legendary to Shakespeare's age, and he also uses her name for the heroine of *The Merchant of Venice* (1598).

BELOW LEFT Geraldine James as Portia with Dustin Hoffman as Shylock, 1989.
BELOW Evelyn Millard as Portia in *Julius Caesar*.

Post (s)
One or more messengers are needed in *Henry VI Parts 2 and 3* (*c*.1594/*c*.1595).

Posthumus
This young leading man in *Cymbeline* (1611) is the somewhat gullible husband of the King's daughter, Imogen, who is the heroine. He is a soldier and fights for Britain against ancient Rome, but is duped into believing that Imogen has been unfaithful. The character of Posthumus is not entirely satisfactorily drawn, and perhaps indicates the struggles of the author with a new type of play, the so-called 'romances', which characterise his last works.

Potpan
A walk-on servant in *Romeo and Juliet* (1597).

Prentice
Either of two minor characters found in *Henry VI Part 2* (*c*.1594), who are actually apprentices and are only walk-on roles.

Priam, King of Troy
This aged and legendary figure is found in *Troilus and Cressida* (*c*.1603). Although he is king of the city which is beseiged by the Greeks, Priam's role is marginal.

Priest (s)
Minor clergymen called for in *Richard III* (*c*.1597) and *Twelfth Night* (1602). Given the period of the former, and the Mediterranean location of the latter, these priests would be Catholic.

Proculeius, Caius
A minor historical figure who is a follower of Octavius Caesar in *Antony and Cleopatra* (1608).

Prologue
An impersonal male figure of indeterminate years, who speaks the opening speech of *Troilus and Cressida* (*c*.1603), *Henry VIII* (1613), and *The Two Noble Kinsmen* (*c*.1613). (See also Chorus.)

Prospero
One of Shakespeare's most evocative figures, Prospero is the central character in the last play which is wholly the playwright's, *The Tempest* (1611). He is a man of mature years who is now living in exile as the ruler of a magical island, having formerly been Duke of Milan. He has been deposed as Duke by his brother Antonio, who falls under Prospero's power as one of a group shipwrecked on the island. A close reading of *The Tempest* reveals that Prospero is not entirely a pleasant character. Although he loves his daughter Miranda, who is on the island with him, he is rather stern and remote as a parent. Prospero is a sorcerer, and his devotion to magic has led him to neglect his duties as the ruler of Milan, leading to the usurpation by Antonio. The magic art of Prospero is displayed as theatrical art on three occasions: the harpy's banquet, the marriage masque, and the presentation of Ferdinand and Miranda in the cave playing chess. Prospero is the 'director' of these spectacles, assisted by his beloved spirit companion Ariel, who acts as 'stage manager'. Prospero is a highly philosophical character. He describes his theatrical art in terms which infer termination and death.

Our revels now are ended. These our actors,
As I foretold you, were all spirits, and
Are melted into air, into thin air;
And, like the baseless fabric of this vision,
The cloud-capped towers, the gorgeous
    palaces,
The solemn temples, the great globe itself,
Yea, all which it inherit, shall dissolve,
And, like this insubstantial pageant faded,
Leave not a wrack behind. We are stuch stuff
As dreams are made on; and our little life
Is rounded with a sleep . . .

Scholars and theatre practitioners have interpreted Prospero, and in particular the above speech, as Shakespeare's farewell to his career in the theatre. The numerous father-daughter relationships of the last plays, and the recurring theme of the reconciliation of families, seem to pre-figure his return to Stratford, and to his estranged wife Anne, and their two

Derek Jacobi as Prospero with Mark Rylance as Ariel, 1982/83.

daughters, Susannah and Judith. This view is speculative, especially as Shakespeare did continue to do some later writing for the stage, but the power of an autobiographical interpretation of *The Tempest* is compelling, and is reinforced by Prospero's words:

> . . . I'll break my staff,
> Bury it certain fathoms in the earth,
> And deeper than did ever plummet sound
> I'll drown my book.

At the end, Prospero gives Ariel his freedom, blesses the marriage of Miranda to Ferdinand, the son of his enemy, Alonso, King of Naples (both of whom were in the shipwreck), renounces his magic powers and makes plans to return to Milan. But he remains a melancholy man, sad to leave his art, his island and Ariel, and depressed by the irredeemable evil in his spirit slave, Caliban, and his brother, Antonio. Speaking the epilogue directly to the audience, Prospero says:

> And my ending is despair,
> Unless it be relieved by prayer,
> Which pierces so, that it assaults,
> Mercy itself, and frees all faults.
> As you from crimes would pardoned be,
> Let your indulgence set me free.

Proteus

One of the title roles in *The Two Gentlemen of Verona* (c.1598), Proteus is a romantic and handsome young man but he is lacking in moral fibre. He betrays his love, Julia, by falling in love with Silvia, who is the bethrothed of his friend Valentine, the other 'gentleman' of the title. Proteus attempts to rape Silvia and contemplates violence against Valentine, but is brought to a better awareness of virtue. Forgiveness and a double marriage are the conclusion of this unsatisfactory play.

Proteus with Silvia and Valentine, by C. Walter Hodges.

Provost

This marginal figure in *Measure For Measure* (1604) is the warden of a prison where Claudio, the hero, is imprisoned.

Publius

Minor character in *Titus Andronicus* (*c*.1594), the son of Marcus Andronicus.

Publius

A very minor figure in *Julius Caesar* (1599), who is a witness to the assassination of the title character.

Puck

This fanciful fairy is also known as Robin Goodfellow, and is a principal character in *A Midsummer Night's Dream* (1598). Puck is a young male spirit who can fly. He is the chief aide to Oberon, the Fairy King, whose orders he gets very mixed up. Puck is comical as well as supernatural, but there are faint overtones of evil in his character which tend to pass unremarked in production.

Pyrrhus

A legendary Greek warrior in *Troilus and Cressida* (*c*.1603), he is a secondary character, described as the son of Achilles. Pyrrhus kills the aged King of Troy, Priam.

Q

Queen

Three minor characters known simply as 'Queen' in *The Two Noble Kinsmen* (*c*.1613), who petition Duke Theseus at his wedding.

Queen of Britain

This secondary character in *Cymbeline* (1611) is a stereotyped wicked stepmother. She intends that her stepdaughter, Imogen, shall marry her son Cloten, who is a dull clod. Imogen, King Cymbeline's daughter, elopes with and marries Posthumus instead. The Queen's lack of a name indicates her relatively unimportant role, which diminishes as the play progresses, and the audience later hears she has died.

Quickly, Mistress

A well-observed townswoman who is found in *The Merry Wives of Windsor* (*c*.1597), *Henry IV Parts 1 and 2* (1598/1600) and *Henry V* (*c*.1599). In *Merry Wives* Mistress Quickly is the housekeeper of Dr Caius, a French doctor and one of the suitors to the young Anne

Mickey Rooney as Puck, in Max Reinhardt's 1935 film.

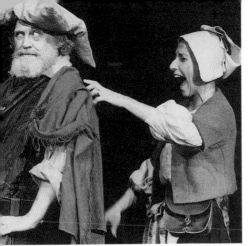

Miriam Karlin as Mistress Quickly with Joss Ackland as Sir John Falstaff, 1982.

Page. She is depicted as a silly servant who attempts to further the wooing of the three suitors to Anne, and is a general busybody of mature years, a typical character of small-town life in Elizabethan times. In the histories, however, we find a rather different person. Sometimes she is known as Mistress Quickly, sometimes merely as Hostess, since she runs the Boar's Head Tavern in Eastcheap, where Sir John Falstaff and his cronies sojourn and the Prince of Wales is a regular customer. She is a good-hearted if simple woman, whose affection for the rascal Falstaff withstands his constant borrowing of money from her. In *Henry V*, it is the hostess who gives the moving description of the death of Falstaff. She is by now married to Pistol, a follower of Falstaff. The setting of the histories is medieval, and Mistress Quickly is here found not in a small town but in an urban environment, which is also quasi-criminal.

Quince, Peter
One of the delightful 'rude mechanicals' in *A Midsummer Night's Dream* (1598), by trade a carpenter. With his friends, he is producing a play for the Duke's wedding. Quince has the task of director of the unintentionally comic *Pyramus and Thisbe*. The performance of this by the artisans is given at the end of the *Dream*, and aside from the enjoyment it provides, this section is also interesting as a play-within-a-play, a device also found in *Hamlet* (c.1602). Quince acts out the tasks of a real Elizabethan troupe director, having written the play and also organised the props and staging.

Quintus
Minor figure, a son of the title character in *Titus Andronicus* (c.1594).

Philip Locke as Quince with the other mechanicals, 1970.

R

Rambures, Lord
A minor French nobleman in *Henry V* (*c*.1599).

Rannius
A silent figure in *Antony and Cleopatra* (1608), an attendant on Enobarbus.

Ratcliffe, Sir Richard
Historical figure who is a follower of the title character in *Richard III* (*c*.1597), and carries out several executions on his behalf.

Reapers
Male dancers in *The Tempest* (1611), who perform a dance with nymphs at the marriage celebration of Miranda and Ferdinand.

Rebels
Extras who take part in the rebellion of Jack Cade in *Henry VI Part 2* (*c*.1594).

Regan
A leading character in *King Lear* (1608), Regan is one of the two wicked daughters of the elderly King. She and her sister Goneril at first act in accord in abusing their father, but gradually the two women become enemies, due to their shared lust for Edmund, the bastard. Unlike Albany, her elder sister's husband, Regan's husband, the Duke of Cornwall, is equally vicious. Regan follows his lead in the onstage blinding of the elderly Duke of Gloucester, in one of the strongest and most unpleasant scenes in Shakespeare. Although Regan is despicable, she is more a follower of her sister and husband than an initiator. She is finally poisoned by the jealous Goneril.

Reignier, Duke of Anjou and King of Naples
Although this historical character in *Henry VI Part 1* (*c*.1592) has a minor role, he is the father of Margaret of Anjou, the principal female character in the trilogy. Like other French noblemen in the history plays, Reignier, also referred to as René, is depicted as fairly incompetent.

Reynaldo
A minor character in *Hamlet* (*c*.1602), who is follower of the King's minister Polonius.

Reynaldo
A minor figure in *All's Well That Ends Well* (*c*.1603), the steward in the household of the Countess of Rossillion.

Richard II, King of England (1367-1400)
The historical Richard was 33 when he died, and this is the impression one gets from *Richard II* (*c*.1597). The story is constructed on a rise and fall pattern; we witness the rise of Henry Bolingbroke, his usurpation of the throne, and the simultaneous decline, and finally murder, of Richard. Although Richard is a weak ruler, who is vain and arrogant, Shakespeare elicits a gradually increasing sympathy for him as, through his sufferings, Richard comes to a better

Herbert Beerbohm-Tree as Richard II.

awareness of himself and his duties. His adversary, Henry, is by no means a villain; he has a legitimate grievance and means to press it (see Bolingbroke).

The central dilemma of the play is concerned with the medieval concept of the divine right of kings, an idea which originated with the Old Testament, and according to which the monarch who succeeds to the throne by correct hereditary descent can never be legitimately deposed, no matter how badly he or she may behave. The ruler is seen as God's annointed, and to depose or murder him was to bring down the Almighty's vengeance on generations yet unborn, in the form of war, pestilence, starvation and the like. The murder of Richard II touches off a long period of civil and foreign wars and other misfortunes which is the subject of Shakespeare's English history plays. Shakespeare's age still held firm to the concept of the divine right of kings, and a rigid order of succession to an hereditary crown. His English and Roman history plays stress his strong belief in civil order. Elizabeth I, in whose reign *Richard II* was written, was known to be very sensitive both about the reign and about Shakespeare's play. The dramatist's source was Holinshed's massive *Chronicles*, and Shakespeare's use of his material is fairly accurate, unlike *Richard III* (*c*.1597).

Richard II is depicted as a sensitive and poetic person, who enjoys posing; his characteristic style of speech is eloquent and mannered. Richard's vivid imagination and increasing introspection are qualities which come to fruition in *Hamlet* (*c*.1602) a few years later. He is perhaps the author's most lyrical character; unlike Hamlet he never speaks in prose. In recognising that all has turned against him, Richard speaks one of the author's great passages:

> Of comfort no man speak.
> Let's talk of graves, of worms and epitaphs;
> Make dust our paper, and with rainy eyes

RIGHT Jeremy Irons plays Richard II, 1986.

David Garrick as Richard III, engraving after the painting by William Hogarth.

Write sorrow on the bosom of the earth.
Let's choose executors and talk of wills –
And yet not so; for what can we bequeath
Save our deposed bodies to the ground?
Our lands, our lives, and all are
    Bolingbroke's,
And nothing can we call our own but death
And that small model of the barren earth
Which serves as paste and cover to our bones.
For God's sake let us sit upon the ground
And tell sad stories of the death of kings –
How some have been deposed, some slain in
    war,
Some haunted by the ghosts they have
    deposed,
Some poisoned by their wives, some sleeping
    killed,
All murdered. For within the hollow crown
That rounds the mortal temple of a king
Keeps Death his court . . .

Although Richard talks about himself repeatedly, it is interesting that he has no soliloquy until Act V, Scene 5. In this late speech, the King is in his prison cell and prepares himself for death in dialogue which is more subdued and humble. His character has been enobled by suffering and he has become resigned to his fate; 'I wasted time, and now time doth waste me'. Yet when his attackers burst into the prison to murder him, he fights bravely, and manages to kill two of them before he dies. His end is certainly better than his beginning, which is the true point of tragedy.

Richard III, King of England (1452–85)

Like *Richard II* (*c*.1597), *Richard III* (*c*.1597) is constructed on a rise and fall pattern. In this case, however, the pattern is found within one character, Richard, Duke of Gloucester, later King. The character appears in a younger guise in *Henry VI Parts 2 and 3* (*c*.1594/*c*.1595), where he is a ruthless young warrior who is even then capable of the macabre gesture. As others recount their deeds in battle, he throws down the head of Somerset, calling on the corpse to tell what Richard did. The character of Richard is a 'machiavel', one who revels in evil; his black humour is very much a part of the early character, as well as of the more fully developed figure in *Richard III*. His alleged humpback is repeatedly referred to in all three plays in which he figures, and this deformity of body is a metaphor for his deformity of soul. He is also frequently described by ugly animal imagery.

The character of Richard has enormous stage energy and charisma. He needs it; his is the second longest role in the whole of Shakespeare, second only to Hamlet in the number of lines. Richard murders his way to the throne, but his energy lags once it is achieved. Although he himself believes that his deformity renders him unattractive to women, he finds out otherwise when he woos Lady Anne Neville, whose husband he has murdered, over the coffin of her father-in-law, Henry VI, whom he has also despatched. This scene finds its parallel much later in the play when, his wife having been killed on his orders, he now attempts to woo his absent niece, Princess Elizabeth of York, through the proxy of her mother, Queen Elizabeth (whose other children he has murdered). This highly ambiguous scene suggests that the mother too is not entirely immune to him. In fact Richard is to an extent defined as a character by his relationship with the four royal women in the play. His mother, the old Duchess, curses him, as does his former adversary, Queen Margaret. *Richard III* is unusual amongst the histories in giving more prominence to the female roles.

Richard III, again like *Richard II* is concerned with the concept of the divine right of kings. Richard III lacks the legitimacy which royal status confers, as he is an usurper, whereas Richard II, for all his faults, is the recipient of God's endorsement. Shakespeare telescopes the history of 85 years, from the murder of the lawful king in 1400 until the death of Richard III at the Battle of Bosworth Field in 1485. Including the two parts of *Henry IV* and the *Henry VI* trilogy, he encompasses six reigns and the brief moment of the uncrowned boy king, Edward V. Richard III has many

Anthony Sher as a particularly malevolent Richard III, 1984/85.

enemies, several of whom he personally murders and others whom he causes to be despatched, including women and children. His real enemy, however, is God, who is personified by Henry Tudor, Earl of Richmond, the victor of Bosworth Field and the founder of the Tudor dynasty. This character makes a very late appearance in the play, and one which is highly symbolic.

The presence of God is also implied in the scene on the eve of battle where Richmond prays before going to sleep, and eight ghostly visitations then cross the stage. These represent Richard's murdered victims, and they visit first Richard, whom they curse, and secondly Richmond, to bless him. This use of the supernatural is highly unusual in the English history plays, and indeed is the most elaborate use of ghosts anywhere in the canon. These visitations are, in effect, God calling Richard to account; he starts up out of his nightmare, calling on Christ, and begins to talk of conscience for the first and only time in the play. His long soliloquy ends:

My conscience hath a thousand several tongues,
And every tongue brings in a several tale,
And every tale condemns me for a villain.
Perjury, perjury, in the highest degree.
Murder, stern murder, in the direst degree,
All several sins, all used in each degree,
Throng to the bar, crying all 'Guilty! Guilty!'

Ian McKellen as Richard III, 1990.

I shall despair. There is no creature loves me;
And if I die, no soul will pity me.
Nay, wherefore should they, since that I myself
Find in myself no pity to myself?
Methought the souls of all that I had murdered
Came to my tent, and every one did threat
Tomorrow's vengeance on the head of Richard.

Richard somewhat recovers his self-control to meet the battle and fights bravely, even after he loses his horse. The stage directions imply that Richard is killed onstage by Richmond, unlike Macbeth, whom Macduff despatches offstage.

The character of Richard III was first played by Richard Burbage, and from the start it was always one of the author's most popular plays. In 1700, the playwright and actor Colley Cibber introduced a radically altered version of the text, which held the stage for generations and was even used in part in Olivier's famous film version. David Garrick, John Philip Kemble, Edmund Kean, Henry Irving, John Barrymore, Laurence Olivier, Anthony Sher and Ian McKellen are among many who have played Richard.

Richmond, Henry Tudor, Earl of (later King Henry VII) (1457-1509)

This secondary figure in *Richard III* (*c*.1597) is rather a cardboard character, but is of immense importance to the conclusion of the play. Richmond is quite literally the white knight in shining armour who defeats the evil Richard at the Battle of Bosworth Field. We first meet him briefly prior to the death of Richard when, on the eve of the battle, his and Richard's prayers bring forth the procession of ghosts who curse Richard and then individually cross to Richmond's tent to bless him. This spectacle reinforces the point that Richmond is God's agent of vengeance on the bloodthirsty tyrant. Richmond's oration on the age of peace, which his victory and marriage to Princess Elizabeth of York will usher in, closes the play, and ends the Wars of the Roses with which Shakespeare's English history plays have been concerned. Richmond's final speech also includes a complimentary reference to his future granddaughter, Elizabeth I. His character is entirely religious and symbolic in nature. He also appears very briefly as a child in *Henry VI Part 3* (*c*.1595).

Rivers, Anthony Woodville, Earl of

This marginal character is found in *Henry VI Part 3* (*c*.1595) and *Richard III* (*c*.1597), and is killed by the latter. Rivers is the brother of Queen Elizabeth Woodville Grey.

Robert

Silent walk-on, a servant in *The Merry Wives of Windsor* (*c*.1597).

Roderigo

This young man is an important secondary character in *Othello* (1604). Roderigo is a gullible Venetian aristocrat who is being exploited financially by the villain, Iago, into thinking that he has some chance of wooing Othello's wife, Desdemona. Roderigo descends to attempted murder through the machinations of Iago.

Roman

Three supernumeraries who are soldiers in *Coriolanus* (1608).

Romeo

One of the most famous figures in literature, whose very name has become a byword for 'lover', he is, of course, one of the title characters in *Romeo and Juliet* (1597). At first this young Veronese nobleman is in love with Rosaline, an offstage character, but when, with some other youths, he gatecrashes a masked ball being held by Juliet's family, he falls immediately in love with the heroine. His first impression of her is a justly famed passage:

O, she doth teach the torches to burn bright!
It seems she hangs upon the cheek of night
As a rich jewel in an Ethiop's ear –
Beauty too rich for use, for earth too dear!
So shows a snowy dove trooping with crows
As yonder lady o'er her fellows shows.
The measure done, I'll watch her place of
   stand

Charles Kemble plays Romeo, 1819.

And touching hers, make blessed my rude
   hand.
Did my heart love till now? Forswear it, sight!
For I ne'er saw true beauty till this night.

Romeo begins to mature from this
moment. He marries Juliet in secret,
opposing the wishes of their families and
friends. Although he tries to be
reconciled with his world, circumstances
forbid it, and the young lovers die
together. Most of the great actors of the
past have played Romeo in their
formative years, and the play has been
filmed many times.

Rosalind

Leading lady in *As You Like It* (1600),
and one of the dramatist's greatest
characters. Rosalind is both a teacher and
a learner about love. She loves Orlando,
and woos him in the guise of a youth
named Ganymede when they meet in the
Forest of Arden. With the freedom that a
breeches role provides for certain
heroines in the comedies, Rosalind is able
to act in an independent manner in a
man's world. Playing both a man and
woman simultaneously, Rosalind is able
to instruct in love not only Orlando, but

ABOVE Katharine Hepburn as Rosalind, 1950.
LEFT Leonard Whiting as Romeo with Olivia Hussey's Juliet in Zeffirelli's 1968 film.
BELOW LEFT Juliet Stevenson as Rosalind and Hilton McRae as Orlando, 1987.

also Phebe, a shepherdess. Rosalind is a witty and resourceful heroine, and the loving companion of her cousin Celia. It is the machinations of Rosalind which result in the four marriages with which the comedy closes, and in a rather unusual departure from custom, Shakespeare assigns to her the epilogue. Many well-known actresses have taken this role, from Peg Woffington in the eighteenth century, to Lillie Langtry in the nineteenth and Vanessa Redgrave in the twentieth.

Rosaline
A secondary character in *Love's Labour's Lost* (*c*.1598), who is the beloved of Berowne and an attendant on the Princess of France.

Rosencrantz
Together with his friend Guildenstern, this courtier is a childhood friend of the title character in *Hamlet* (*c*.1602). The two young men are villains, and are so alike that they almost form a unit.

Ross, William de
This minor historical figure is found in *Richard II* (*c*.1597), where he is a follower of Henry Bolingbroke.

Ross, or Rosse, Thane of
A Scottish nobleman in *Macbeth* (1606).

Rossillion, Countess of
A major character in *All's Well That Ends Well* (*c*.1603), she is the mother of the hero, Bertram, and the guardian of Helena, the exemplary woman who loves him. The wise Countess comments on the action of the play from her estate at Rossillion. It has been suggested that Shakespeare modelled her on Mary Sidney, Countess of Pembroke, an

important Elizabethan patroness of the arts and sister to the poet Sir Philip Sidney. The Countess Rossillion's character shines in an otherwise unsympathetic play; Bernard Shaw called hers the most beautiful old woman's part ever written. It was the last Shakespearean role taken by Dame Peggy Ashcroft, who gave a memorable performance with the Royal Shakespeare Company.

Rotherham, Thomas, Archbishop of York

Historical figure and minor character in *Richard III* (*c*.1597), where he appears as a friend of Queen Elizabeth, wife of Edward IV. In some modern editions Rotherham is omitted and his lines given to Cardinal Bourchier, following the precedent of sixteenth-century quarto editions.

Rugby, John

Minor servant in *The Merry Wives of Windsor* (*c*.1597).

Rumour

This allegorical figure functions as a chorus in *Henry IV Part 2* (1600). He introduces the play.

Rutland, Edmund, Earl of

This minor historical figure appears as a child in *Henry VI Part 3* (*c*.1595); he is the son of Richard, Duke of York, the Yorkist claimant to the throne, and is killed by Clifford in revenge for the death of his father.

S

Sailor

Supernumeraries designated as sailor(s) are called for in *Hamlet* (*c*.1602), *Othello* (1604), and *Pericles, Prince of Tyre* (*c*.1609).

Salerio and Solanio

Two young aristocratic Venetian gentlemen who have small parts in *The Merchant of Venice* (*c*.1598). They are

Peggy Ashcroft as the Countess of Rossillion, 1981.

friends of Antonio, the merchant of the title, and are so alike as to function almost as a unit, normally appearing together.

Salisbury, John Montague, Earl of

Minor character, a historical figure who is a supporter of *Richard II* (*c*.1597).

Salisbury, Richard Neville, Earl of

Historical nobleman found in *Henry VI Part 2* (*c*.1594). Although he is reminded by King Henry of his allegiance, Salisbury announces his support of the Yorkist cause. He is, however, distinguished from the ambitious nobles around him.

Salisbury, Thomas Montague, Earl of

This minor character is an historical figure in *Henry VI Part 1* (*c*.1592) and *Henry V* (*c*.1599), an English general.

Salisbury, William Longsword, Earl of
Historical character who leads a group of rebels against the title character in *King John* (*c*. 1595).

Sampson
A servant of the Capulets in *Romeo and Juliet* (1597).

Sands (Sandys), Lord William
Minor historical character at the court of *Henry VIII* (1613).

Saturninus
This vengeful character becomes emperor of Rome in *Titus Andronicus* (*c*.1594) with the help of the title character, but turns against Titus.

Satyrs
Twelve men dressed as satyrs perform a dance in *The Winter's Tale* (1611) in a mini-masque.

Say, James Finnes, Lord
Historical figure in *Henry VI Part 2* (*c*.1594). A courageous man, he is Treasurer of England, but is captured by the rebels and Jack Cade and killed by them.

Scales, Lord Thomas de
Historical but minor figure in *Henry VI Part 2* (*c*.1594). He is Commander of the Tower of London, and helps to drive Jack Cade and the rebels from the capital.

Scarus
A follower of Antony at the Battle of Actium in *Antony and Cleopatra* (1608), who reports on the disastrous rout of the lovers.

Schoolmaster
A minor character in *The Two Noble Kinsmen* (*c*.1613) by Shakespeare and John Fletcher.

Scout
A walk-on in *Henry VI Part 1* (*c*.1592), he is a French soldier who brings news of the English approach.

Scribe
A minor functionary at the divorce trial of Queen Katharine in *Henry VIII* (1613).

Scrivener
A minor official in *Richard III* (*c*.1597) who copies records.

Scroop (Scrope) Sir Stephen
Historical figure found in *Richard II* (*c*.1597), a minor character and supporter of the King.

Scroop (Scrope), Henry
Historical figure found in *Henry V* (*c*.1599), a traitor who intends to kill the King, but instead is executed on Henry's orders before his expedition leaves for France. Scroop is one of three conspirators, all with small roles.

Scroop, Richard, Archbishop of York
Historical figure who appears in Henry IV Parts 1 and 2 (1598/1600). Scroop is the leader of the rebels against Henry Bolingbroke, the future Henry IV, and in Part 2 is sentenced to death.

Sea Captain
A minor part in *Henry VI Part 2* (*c*.1594).

Sea Captain
A walk-on who rescues Viola from the shipwreck in the opening scene of *Twelfth Night* (1602).

Seacoal, George
A minor character, a member of the night watch in *Much Ado About Nothing* (*c*.1599) and one of several humorous rustics.

Sebastian
The name taken by Julia when she goes into disguise in *The Two Gentlemen of Verona* (*c*.1598).

Sebastian
A secondary character in *Twelfth Night* (1602), Sebastian is the twin brother of the principal heroine, Viola. Both are shipwrecked, but we do not meet

Marius Goring as Sebastian with Ursula Jeans as Viola, 1933.

Sebastian until later in the play, when his appearance is a convenient solution to the complications caused by Viola's disguise as a man. Sebastian is an upright and pleasant youth and makes a satisfactory husband for the second heroine, Olivia, who has unfortunately fallen in love with Viola. Gender is ambiguous in this play.

Sebastian
A secondary character in *The Tempest* (1611) who weakly follows the villain, Antonio, although Sebastian's character is reclaimed.

Second Murderer
Male figures are needed to fill this function in *Henry VI Part 2* (c.1594), *Richard III* (c.1597), and *Macbeth* (1606).

Secretary
Several court functionaries are needed in *Henry VIII* (1613), who are male figures of indeterminate age.

Seleucus
This historical figure is a minor official in *Antony and Cleopatra* (1608). He is an Egyptian and Treasurer to the Queen, but betrays her to Caesar.

Sempronius
A silent walk-on in *Titus Andronicus* (c.1594).

Sempronius
A minor male figure who is a flatterer of the title character in *Timon of Athens* (c.1604).

Senators
One or more male lawmakers of mature years are needed in *Othello* (1604), *Timon of Athens* (c.1604), *Coriolanus* (1608), and *Cymbeline* (1611).

Sentinel (Sentry)
A walk-on character found in *Henry VI Part 1* (c.1592) and *Antony and Cleopatra* (1608).

Sergeant
A French sergeant is found in *Henry VI Parts 1 and 2* (c.1592/c.1594).

Sergeant
Walk-on in *Henry VI Part 2* (c.1594), who dies in the Cade Rebellion.

Servant
Servants are found in many of Shakespeare's plays and can be cast as

different ages and, in modern productions, as either sex.

Servilius
Servant in *Timon of Athens* (*c*.1604), who is a follower of the title character.

Serving-man
Minor characters found in *Henry VI Part 1* (*c*.1592), *The Taming of the Shrew* (*c*.1594), *Romeo and Juliet* (1597), *The Merchant of Venice* (*c*.1598) and *Coriolanus* (1608).

Servitor
An attendant of Antony in *Antony and Cleopatra* (1608). His and his fellows' deep distress at their master's fate reinforces the fact that Antony is loved.

Sexton
A minor official in *Much Ado About Nothing* (*c*.1599) who, as a scribe, records the proceedings of Dogberry and the night watch.

Justice Shallow in the Quarrel Scene, after T.H. Nicholson.

Seyton
A minor officer who is an attendant on *Macbeth* (1606), and announces to him his wife's death.

Shaa (Shaw), Ralph (or John)
Historical character of minor importance in *Richard III* (*c*.1597), one of two unscrupulous clergymen.

Shadow, Simon
A rustic whom Sir John Falstaff recruits for the King's army in *Henry IV Part 2* (1600). Shadow's symbolic name indicates his thinness.

Shallow, Robert
A country justice of the peace, whose symbolic name indicates his character and inadequate knowledge of the law. Shallow is a talkative old man, who helps Sir John Falstaff recruit soldiers and is somewhat gulled by the fat rascal. He is a sympathetic example of small-town life, whom we also meet in *The Merry Wives of Windsor* (*c*.1597), where his character is less substantial but his part is longer.

Shepherd

An old man in *Henry VI Part 1* (*c*.1592) the father of Joan La Pucelle (Joan of Arc).

Shepherd

An old man in *The Winter's Tale* (1611) who, having discovered Perdita as an infant, has acted as her foster father and raised her to the age of 16, as she appears in part two of the play. He is an endearing rustic.

Sheriff

Male officials of indeterminate years are called for in *Henry VI Part 2* (*c*.1594), *King John* (*c*.1595), *Richard III* (*c*.1597) and *Henry IV Part 1* (1598).

Shylock

This colourful and evocative figure is the leading male character in *The Merchant of Venice* (*c*.1598). He is a Jewish moneylender of mature years, who is a widower with a daughter, Jessica. The undoubted anti-semitism in this play has presented difficult problems of performance in the twentieth century. From Shakespeare's time until the performances of Charles Macklin beginning in 1741, Shylock was played as a comic buffoon. Macklin, however, undertook considerable research into Jewish custom and history, with the result that he acted Shylock seriously, albeit still as a villain. This permanently changed the stage history of the character, especially as Macklin continued to act the role until he was into his ninetieth year. Shylock's action in demanding a bond which promises him one pound of the merchant Antonio's flesh, should he be unable to repay his debt by a certain time, is hard to look upon as anything but villainy. It is also true, however, that Shylock and his community have been treated despicably by the Christians in Venice. Shakespeare was building on existing stereotypes in literature, but as is usual with him, has raised his material far above the source. There is no simple answer to Shylock,

Edmund Kean as Shylock.

but his most celebrated speech reflects the author at his most humane.

. . . I am a Jew. Hath not a Jew eyes? Hath not a Jew hands, organs, dimensions, senses, affections, passions? Fed with the same food, hurt with the same weapons, subject to the same diseases, healed by the same means, warmed and cooled by the same winter and summer, as a Christian is? If you prick us, do we not bleed? If you tickle us, do we not laugh? If you poison us, do we not die? And if you wrong us, shall we not revenge? If we are like you in the rest, we will resemble you in that.

The two characteristics which were assumed in Shakespeare's England to be essentially Jewish are hatred of Christians and the practice of usury, and Shylock's name has become a byword for miserliness. But the author adds to that a man who loves his late wife and his daughter, a man of high intelligence, and one who has been abused by society. Yet he cruelly refuses mercy to Antonio, even for huge sums of money. Shylock's defeat in court is appropriate, but modern auditors must shudder when he is forcibly converted to Christianity and suffers the betrayal of his daughter.

Many great actors have played the role, and although Macklin is not in that category, his contribution to this particular play is immense. The nineteenth century was able to build on that with great performances by Edmund Kean, William Charles Macready, Edwin Booth, Charles Kean, and especially Henry Irving. Although there have been some arresting recent performances, the last great 'romantic' appearance was Laurence Olivier, whose performance in a nineteenth-century style production by Jonathan Miller was Olivier's last role in Shakespeare on the stage. This was presented under his own management at the National Theatre. As his Shylock left the stage in the throes of a heart attack, he left no doubt that the play on this occasion was a tragedy about Shylock.

ABOVE Antony Sher as Shylock, 1987.
BELOW Charles Macklin as Shylock with Jane Pope as Portia.

Sicinius Velutus
See Brutus, Junius.

Silence
This old man is a rural justice of the peace in *Henry IV Part 2* (1600) and, as his comically symbolic name implies, has little to say for himself. He is a cousin of Justice Shallow, and adds a touch of humorous atmosphere.

Silius
Minor soldier in *Antony and Cleopatra* (1608).

Silvia
The more important of the two female leads in *The Two Gentlemen of Verona* (*c*.1598), Silvia is a conventional romantic heroine in what is one of the weaker comedies. She is the object of rivalry between the two gentlemen of the title, Proteus and Valentine.

Silvia with Julia, Proteus and Valentine, engraved by Osborne.

Silvius
This young shepherd, although a small part in *As You Like It* (1600), greatly adds to the texture of life in the forest of Arden. He is in love with a very disdainful miss, Phebe.

Simonides
This dignified secondary character appears in *Pericles, Prince of Tyre* (*c*.1609). Simonides is the King of Pentapolis and the father of Thaisa, who becomes the wife of the title character. Simonides appears only in Act II, but as the play covers many years and many locations, only Pericles is really developed at length. As a noble father figure Simonides has a symbolic importance to the action which is perhaps greater than the character's stage time.

Simpcox, Saunder
Minor rustic character who appears with his wife as walk-ons in *Henry VI Part 2* (*c*.1594), providing a bit of low comedy.

Simple, Peter
Servant to Slender in *The Merry Wives of Windsor* (*c*.1597). He is slow-witted, and is part of the generally affectionate portrayal of small-town life found in this comedy.

Siward, Earl of Northumberland
Historical figure found in *Macbeth* (1606), where he is in an English ally of Malcolm and Macduff against the title character. Siward is an honest and straightforward soldier who courageously bears the death of his son, young Siward.

Slender, Master Abraham
Dull-witted nephew of Justice Shallow in *The Merry Wives of Windsor* (*c*.1597). Master Slender is not only very thin, but utterly lacking in self-confidence. He is a reluctant suitor to Anne Page, but fortunately for her she manages to avoid his feeble suit. Slender is one of several eccentric portraits of small-town figures which distinguish this early farce.

Sir John
A priest who speaks one line in *Richard III* (*c*.1597).

Sly, Christopher
The principal character in the induction scene to *The Taming of the Shrew* (*c*.1594).

LEFT Oscar Ashe as Christopher Sly.

He is a drunken tinker who is found asleep outside an inn and, due to a trick by the locals, wakes up to believe himself really to be a lord. As part of the joke, a troupe of players presents *The Taming of the Shrew*.

Smith the Weaver

Follower of the rebel Jack Cade in *Henry VI Part 2* (*c*.1594). The role of Smith is very small.

Snare

Officer of the sheriff who tries to arrest Sir John Falstaff in *Henry IV Part 2* (1600), a bit part.

Snout, Tom

A tinker and one of the 'rude mechanicals' in *A Midsummer Night's Dream* (1598), a group of artisans who are engaged to present a play for Duke Theseus's wedding. Snout's role is 'wall' in the performance of *Pyramus and Thisbe*.

Snug

A joiner and also one of the 'rude mechanicals' from Athens who present an amateur performance for the Duke's wedding in *A Midsummer Night's Dream* (1598). Snug takes the role of the lion.

LEFT Oscar Ashe as Christopher Sly.

Solanio

See Salerio.

Soldier(s)

Quite a number of soldiers are required in Shakespeare's plays. These are minor male characters of military age. The soldiers are English, French, Greek, Roman or Renaissance and would be costumed as appropriate to each play. They feature in *Henry VI Part 1* (*c*.1592), *Henry VI Part 2* (*c*.1594), *Titus Andronicus* (*c*.1594), *Julius Caesar* (1599), *All's Well That Ends Well* (*c*.1603), *Troilus and Cressida* (*c*.1603), *Timon of Athens* (*c*.1604), *Antony and Cleopatra* (1608), and *Coriolanus* (1608).

Solinus, Duke of Ephesus

A character in *The Comedy of Errors* (*c*.1594) who rules the city where the action takes place. His role is small and purely official.

Somerset, Edmund Beaufort, Duke of

This historical character has a small role in *Henry VI Part 2* (*c*.1594), where he is a Lancastrian supporter. He is the younger brother of John Beaufort, Duke of Somerset, who is found in *Henry VI Part 1* (*c*.1592).

Somerset, John Beaufort, Duke of

This historical figure is a rival to the Duke of York, claimant to the throne, in *Henry VI Part 1* (*c*.1592). This Somerset is depicted as somewhat dishonourable, and figures in the emblematic scene in the Temple Garden in London, where various members of the rival factions pick white or red roses to symbolise their response to the dynastic struggle between the York and Lancaster branches of the Plantagenet family. This scene is entirely fictional, but casts in very effective stage terms the beginning of the Wars of the Roses. Somerset selects a red rose, signifying his allegiance to the house of Lancaster.

Somerset, Duke of
This character in *Henry VI Part 3* (*c*.1595) suggests that Shakespeare may have been somewhat confused by the Somersets, and thus created a composite figure based on Henry and his younger brother Edmund, both of whom were sons of Edmund Beaufort, Duke of Somerset, a character in *Henry VI Part 2* (*c*.1594). All were involved in the Wars of the Roses.

Somerville, Sir John
Minor historical figure in *Henry VI Part 3* (*c*.1595), a follower of Warwick and a rebel against Edward IV.

Son
This young lad, aged about ten, is the son of Macduff and Lady Macduff in *Macbeth* (1606). He appears with his mother (who is also holding an infant) in only one scene, and carries on a lively conversation with her until murderers burst in and attack them. Although a very small part, this child shows wit, intelligence and compassion for his mother, which makes his slaughter by agents of the title character even more heart-rending.

Speed, with Launce, servants to the title characters in *Two Gentlemen*.

Son That Hath Killed His Father
This emblematic character from *Henry VI Part 3* (*c*.1595) is the pendant to the 'father that hath killed his son'. The son in this case begins to loot a corpse which he has killed at the Battle of Towton, but finds it to be his father. This and its matching scene are witnessed by Henry VI and symbolize the particular horror of civil war.

Soothsayer
This minor but symbolically important character is found in *Julius Caesar* (1599), where his function is to warn Caesar to 'beware the Ides of March' (March 15th). He has a second encounter with Caesar, who remarks that the Ides have arrived without harm, to which the soothsayer replies, 'Ay, Caesar, but not gone'. The assassination occurs soon after.

Soothsayer
This minor character is found in *Antony and Cleopatra* (1608) as a follower of Antony. A male seer of mature years, he is probably intended to be a native Egyptian.

Soothsayer
A minor prophet serving the Roman army in *Cymbeline* (1611). The Romans were very superstitious, and so in plays with Roman characters, soothsayers are both atmospherically useful and accurate.

Southwell, John
Historical figure of minor importance in *Henry VI Part 2* (*c*.1594). Southwell is a sorcerer accused of plotting with the Duchess of Gloucester to kill the King. He is arrested.

Speed
This cheeky page is found in *Two Gentlemen of Verona* (*c*.1598). He is an attendant of Valentine, one of the title characters, and is a small part.

Stafford, Lord Humphrey
Bit part in *Henry VI Part 3* (*c*.1595), an adherent of Edward IV.

Stafford, Sir Humphrey
Minor nobleman in *Henry VI Part 2* (*c*.1594). His arrogant handling of the Jack Cade rebellion is counter-productive, and Stafford and his brother are killed in the skirmish which results.

Stafford, Sir William
Historical character in *Henry VI Part 2* (*c*.1594) who is a brother of Sir Humphrey Stafford and attempts to help put down the rebellion of Cade, but is killed with his brother.

Stafford
See Buckingham.

Stanley, Sir John
A minor historical character in *Henry VI Part 2* (*c*.1594), a sympathiser with the disgraced Duchess of Gloucester.

Stanley, Sir Thomas
Historical figure who is a secondary character in *Richard III* (*c*.1597). This nobleman defects decisively from Richard at the Battle of Bosworth Field and goes over to the cause of Richmond, placing Richard's crown on the head of the victorious Richmond, the future Henry VII. Stanley is a man of mature years whose son is an offstage character in the battle.

Stanley, Sir William
A minor historical character found in *Henry VI Part 3* (*c*.1595), who is a supporter of Edward IV and the brother of Thomas and John Stanley, who also appear as characters in the history plays.

Starveling, Robin
A tailor and part of the group of workers who present the amateur play *Pyramus and Thisbe* for the Duke's wedding at the conclusion of *A Midsummer Night's Dream* (1598). Starveling takes the role of Moonshine in the play-within-the-play.

Stephano
Servant of Portia in *The Merchant of Venice* (*c*.1598).

Stephano with Caliban, in *The Tempest*.

Stephano
A drunken attendant on King Alonso of Naples in *The Tempest* (1611). This minor character conspires with Caliban to kill Prospero.

Stranger(s)
Two or three walk-on characters are depicted as visitors to Athens in *Timon of Athens* (*c*.1604). Numbers vary and in the First Folio the second stranger is called Hostilius (see Hostilius).

Strato
A minor Greek soldier who helps Brutus commit suicide in *Julius Caesar* (1599). This historical figure was then taken into the service of Octavius.

Suffolk
See Brandon.

Suffolk, William de la Pole, Earl of, later Duke

Historical character of secondary importance in *Henry VI Parts 1 and 2* (*c*.1592/*c*.1594). This ambitious nobleman negotiates the marriage of Margaret of Anjou with Henry VI, but falls in love with her himself. In the second part of the trilogy, the lovers are parted when the King banishes Suffolk.

Surrey, Thomas Fitzalan, Earl of

This minor historical figure is a follower of the King in *Henry IV Part 2* (1600).

Surrey, Thomas Holland, Duke of

This historical figure is an adherent of the King in *Richard II* (*c*.1597).

Surrey, Thomas Howard, Earl of

Historical character who is a nobleman at court in *Henry VIII* (1613).

Surveyor

A villainous steward to the Duke of Buckingham in *Henry VIII* (1613).

T

Taborer

Minor figure, a musician in *The Two Noble Kinsmen* (*c*.1613) who accompanies a group of dancing women on a drum.

Tailor

A minor comic character in *The Taming of The Shrew* (*c*.1594), who is summoned by Petruchio, supposedly to make a new outfit for his bride.

Talbot, Lord John (d.1453)

An important historical figure who is found in *Henry VI Part 1* (*c*.1592) and represents the best of chivalrous values. This English military hero's career is linked to and contrasted with Joan La Pucelle (Joan of Arc) to the detriment of the Frenchwoman. The death of Talbot, together with his young son, both of

Talbot's army engages with Joan La Pucelle, by C. Walter Hodges.

whom fight bravely, is due to lack of reinforcements and to wrangles on the English side.

Talbot, Young
John Talbot, son of the above, appears briefly in *Henry VI Part I* (*c*.1592). He refuses his father's pleas to flee the hopeless battle and dies to maintain the family honour.

Tamora, Queen of the Goths
This evil woman is a leading character in *Titus Andronicus* (*c*.1594). She is a mature woman with three sons who takes as her lover the Moor Aaron, which, in the context of the play, is seen as a mark of her depravity. At the start of the play they have been captured by Titus, and a cycle of horrendous revenge is set in motion. The climax of this chain of events takes place at a banquet, where Titus serves Tamora the flesh of her murdered sons, before killing her as well. This horrifying play was very popular in its day and is the subject of the only extant contemporary illustration of a Shakespearean play in performance (see page 10). The character of Tamora is melodramatic; she displays extreme lust, vicious violence, and cunning ambition. Her role finds its precursor in the female parts of the Roman tragic writer Seneca, who was much admired by the Elizabethans. Tamora's mode of expression is highly rhetorical, which is one more characteristic taken from Seneca. Greek tragedy was practically unknown in sixteenth-century England and the Elizabethans therefore took as their model the Roman tragedy of Seneca, not realizing that his works were not intended to be acted. The Senecan tragedy which most influenced *Titus* was *Thyestes*.

Taurus, Titus Statilius
Minor historical figure, a military leader under Octavius Caesar in *Antony and Cleopatra* (1608).

RIGHT Sheila Hancock as Tamora, 1981.

Thaliard

A minor character in *Pericles, Prince of Tyre* (*c*.1609), Thaliard is an assassin hired to poison the hero by King Antiochus of Syria, but in the event does not carry out his plan.

Thersites

Legendary character in *Troilus and Cressida* (*c*.1603), a foolish follower of Ajax and Achilles. The constant outbursts of Thersites against all and sundry are hateful, but at times add a funny note to this long and bitter play. He is too cowardly to fight; he is in part a *miles gloriosus* figure of a braggart soldier, but has also been likened to a court jester.

Tearsheet, Doll

A colourful bawd in *Henry IV Part 2* (1600), the lover of Sir John Falstaff. Doll is part of the riotous company at the Boar's Head Tavern, and she is genuinely fond of the fat knight. She is in tears when he departs with the army.

Thaisa

This attractive character is a secondary figure in *Pericles, Prince of Tyre* (*c*.1609). Thaisa is the daughter of King Simonides of Pentapolis, and marries Pericles, a knight. After their daughter Marina is born, Thaisa is believed to have died and been buried at sea. She must age and mature in the course of the lengthy story, as she is miraculously preserved and reappears to be reunited with her husband and daughter. This circumstance is one of the numerous supernatural events which are found in the author's so-called 'late romances'. In these plays, for example *The Winter's Tale* (1611), we find the theme of the reconciliation of families, and frequent father-daughter-mother relationships; Thaisa is a conventionally virtuous and beautiful wife and mother. Her character is original to the play and has no connection with other Thais figures found in classical lore.

Theseus

Theseus, Duke of Athens, is a figure from classical legend whom Shakespeare used on two occasions. A mature man and wise ruler, Theseus is an important character in *A Midsummer Night's Dream* (1598). His impending marriage to Hippolyta, Queen of the Amazons, is the starting point of the comedy, and the solemnisation of this rite is the conclusion. He finds himself at the beginning in the unpleasant position of having to impose a harsh penalty on Hermia, should she refuse to marry according to her father's wishes. In this incident, and in other references in the play, it is conjectured that Theseus is a metaphor for Elizabeth I. Theseus attempts to mediate but, failing that, he is committed to carrying out the law. Queen Elizabeth is thought possibly to have been present at the premiere, when the play was presented to celebrate a marriage of the nobility. The *Dream* concludes with the play-within-a-play, in which the kind and tolerant characteristics of Theseus, as the person in whose honour it is performed, are manifested.

Theseus
In his second use of this classical character, Shakespeare places the Duke of Athens in *The Two Noble Kinsmen* (*c*.1613), which he co-authored with John Fletcher and which was not published until well after his own death. In this play Theseus is again a wise ruler. It is conjectured that Shakespeare wrote Acts 1 and 5, and it is in those sections that the character of Theseus is the more prominent, although he remains a secondary figure.

Thidias
Minor character who functions as a diplomatic messenger for Octavius Caesar in *Antony and Cleopatra* (1608).

Third Murderer
A minor character hired by the hero in *Macbeth* (1606).

Thurio
A secondary character in *The Two Gentlemen of Verona* (*c*.1598). Thurio is a foolish rival to Valentine, one of the heroes, for the love of Silvia, whose father, the Duke, has chosen Thurio as her husband. At one stage in the play Thurio arrives below Silvia's window with musicians, who perform one of Shakespeare's noted songs, 'Who is Silvia?' Given the chance at the end to fight Valentine for Silvia, Thurio fearfully declines.

Timandra
See Phrynia.

Time
An allegorical figure, who is found in *The Winter's Tale* (1611) in the function of a chorus. Time appears only at the beginning of Act IV where, speaking alone on the stage, he informs the audience that 16 years have now passed, and the action has moved to Bohemia. To avoid confusing the audience as to who he is, a theatre performance would probably depict him as a conventional old man in a timeless robe holding an hourglass, an obvious attribute of time. Time's language is different from the rest of the text, in that he speaks in rhyming couplets, which helps to place him outside the action of the play.

Timon
This distinguished character is the title character in *Timon of Athens* (*c*.1604). Timon is a benevolent Athenian nobleman, who becomes misanthropic and disillusioned with the world when his generosity results in his financial ruin and abandonment by his false friends. Timon withdraws into the wilderness, inveighing against humanity, and dies, possibly by suicide. His character displays extremes of goodness and hatred. This bleak morality play has elements of tragedy, but also elements of social comment and satire. It is generally agreed that the whole play is not by Shakespeare, and recent scholarship cites Thomas Middleton as the co-author. There is no record of an early performance and the first publication was the First Folio of 1623. An experimental and ambiguous play, *Timon of Athens* is seldom produced today, although the Royal Shakespeare Company presented an interesting studio production, rendered in Japanese style, with Richard Pasco as Timon. More

ABOVE Richard Pasco as Timon, 1981.

huge ass's head. His brief romance with Titania is, therefore, a classic case of 'beauty and the beast'. Bottom is not quite sure he wants to stay with her, but Titania invokes her magic power.

Out of this wood do not desire to go:
I am a spirit of no common rate;
The summer still doth tend upon my state;
And I do love thee: therefore go with me.
I'll give thee fairies to attend on thee;
And they shall fetch thee jewels from the
  deep,
And sing, while thou on pressed flowers dost
  sleep:
And I will purge thy mortal grossness so,
That thou shalt like an airy spirit go.
Peaseblossom! Cobweb! Moth! and
  Mustardseed!

recently a North American production was seen at the Ontario Shakespeare Festival in Canada, which was directed by Michael Langham and starred Brian Bedford as Timon. This was re-staged for Broadway in 1993. Langham's production had interesting under-scoring with music by Duke Ellington. Both director and star received 'Tony' nominations.

Titania
The Queen of Fairies, a leading character in *A Midsummer Night's Dream* (1598). Her character is enjoyable in even the most dismal performance, as she appeals so greatly to our imagination. Titania has fallen out with her husband, Oberon, the King of the Fairies, and he casts a magic spell over her, with the result that she falls temporarily in love with Nick Bottom, the Weaver, who is in the enchanted woods rehearsing a play for the Duke's wedding with a band of local artisans. Bottom has likewise fallen foul of Oberon's spell and has developed a

RIGHT Vivien Leigh plays Titania, 1937.

The character of Titania is graceful in movement, as well as young and beautiful; she is imperious and flamboyant in manner and speech. As her character is supernatural, a great deal of stylisation is needed in production to conform to the magical quality of the text.

Titinius

This minor historical character is a colleague of Cassius in *Julius Caesar* (1599). He is with him at the Battle of Philippi and, finding his master dead, runs on Cassius's sword.

Titus Andronicus

This larger-than-life Roman general is the title character of Shakespeare's early attempt at tragedy, *Titus Adronicus* (c.1594). He is at first depicted as an admirable patriot, but his extreme sense of honour leads him to kill one of his own sons, and he also allows the ritual murder of a son of Tamora, Queen of the Goths. A horrendous cycle of violence and revenge ensues, the low points of which are the rape and horrible mutilation of Titus' daughter, Lavinia, and his own killing of her in response to a warped sense of family honour. He kills and cooks the remaining two sons of Tamora and serves them to her at a banquet, before killing their mother. The character of this old man sinks to a savagery which is only partially explained by his growing madness.

This incredible play was extremely popular when it was first written and for a period of about 30 years, but thereafter for about three and a half centuries it was, understandably, among the most neglected of the dramatist's plays. In the nineteenth century, it had a revival in Britain due to the popularity of the black American actor Ira Aldridge (d.1867) as Aaron the Moor, a role which Aldridge played throughout the capitals of Europe. The most notable twentieth-century production was that which Peter Brook staged for the Royal Shakespeare Company in 1955, with Laurence Olivier as Titus and Vivien Leigh as Lavinia.

Brian Cox as Titus Andronicus, 1987.

Titus

A minor servant in *Timon of Athens* (c.1604).

Topas

Name taken by Feste in *Twelfth Night* (1602), when he disguises himself as a Puritan cleric and visits Malvolio in prison.

Torchbearers

These silent walk-ons accompany Romeo and the masquers to Capulet's banquet and ball in *Romeo and Juliet* (1597).

Touchstone

An important character in *As You Like It* (1600), Touchstone is the court jester and a follower of Rosalind and Celia, with whom the story is largely concerned. Officially an attendant on Celia's father, the wicked Duke Frederick, Touchstone loyally follows the two girls when they flee to the forest of Arden to escape the Duke's anger. Touchstone is a highly intellectual and witty character, and much of his dialogue carries the burden of an exposition of the play's courtly themes. Principal among these is his discussion with Corin, a shepherd, in which the relative merits of city versus

Kenneth Branagh as Touchstone with Richard Easton as Jaques, 1988.

country life are expounded. Touchstone's courtship of the shepherdess Audrey is one of four variations on the theme of love which lead to the multiple weddings at the close of the comedy. The role was probably originally acted by Robert Armin, of Shakespeare's company.

Townsmen of St Albans
Extras in *Henry VI Part 2* (*c*.1594).

Tranio
Comic servant to Lucentio, with whom he temporarily changes place in *The Taming of the Shrew* (*c*.1594). These characters function in the subplot of the wooing of Bianca.

Traveller
Either of two walk-ons in *Henry IV Part 1* (1598), who fall victim to highway robbery at the hands of Falstaff and his cohorts.

Travers
A retainer of the Earl of Northumberland in *Henry IV Part 2* (1600).

Trebonius, Gaius
Minor historical character found in *Julius Caesar* (1599), who is a politician in favour with Caesar but becomes one of the plotters against him.

Tressel
An attendant on Lady Anne Neville in *Richard III* (*c*.1597), when she accompanies the corpse of her father-in-law, Henry VI.

Tribune(s)
Minor Roman officials found in *Titus Andronicus* (*c*.1594), *Coriolanus* (1608), and *Cymbeline* (1611).

Trinculo
Jester to King Alonso of Naples in *The Tempest* (1611). Trinculo is a drunken buffoon who takes part in the abortive plot to kill Prospero.

Troilus
Legendary knight and one of the title characters in *Troilus and Cressida* (*c*.1603). He is a Trojan prince and the lover of the faithless heroine, Cressida. Troilus is self-deluded both as a warrior and a lover and is thus something of a typical romantic hero. His place in Shakespeare's source, Homer, is relatively minor, but the playwright has been further inspired by medieval sources.

Tubal
Friend of Shylock, the Jewish usurer, who is the principal character in *The Merchant of Venice* (*c*.1598). Tubal is also a Jew, and although his character is minor, it adds atmosphere to the conflicting Jewish and Christian elements of society in Venice.

Tutor
A walk-on character in *Henry VI Part 3* (*c*.1595), who is the instructor of Rutland, the son of the Yorkist claimant to the throne.

Tybalt
Young knight with a small but pivotal role in *Romeo and Juliet* (1597). He is a cousin of the heroine and his personality is belligerent. He kills Mercutio, thus

inciting Romeo to revenge by killing Tybalt.

Tyrell, Sir James
Minor historical character found in *Richard III* (*c*.1597), where his villainy encompasses the murder of the two little princes in the Tower of London, on the orders of Richard. His complicity in the actual death of the children is, however, conjectural.

U

Ulysses
This legendary character is an important figure in *Troilus and Cressida* (*c*.1603). He is a mature and rational man, one of the Greek commanders in the Trojan War.

Ursula
Woman of indeterminate years, a silent walk-on who is an attendant on Silvia in *The Two Gentlemen of Verona* (*c*.1598).

Ursula
Lively servant of one of the two heroines, Hero, in *Much Ado About Nothing* (*c*.1599). Her role is mainly decorative.

Urswick, Christopher
Historical but minor figure in *Richard III* (*c*.1597), who is a follower of Richard's rival, Richmond.

Usher
A walk-on in *Coriolanus* (1608), a servant who is often dropped from productions.

V

Valentine
Silent walk-on in *Titus Andronicus* (*c*.1594).

Valentine
One of the title characters in *The Two Gentlemen of Verona* (*c*.1598). Valentine is in love with the main heroine, Silvia, but the other 'gentleman', Proteus, tries to steal her. Valentine is sent into exile through the machinations of his so-called friend, Proteus. Although Valentine is somewhat inept as a lover, a happy resolution is reached in this early comedy.

Valentine
This minor character is a young courtier, and follower of Duke Orsino in *Twelfth Night* (1602).

Valeria
Walk-on character who is a friend and attendant of the hero's wife in *Coriolanus* (1608).

Valerius
Minor character who is a friend of the title characters in *The Two Noble Kinsmen* (*c*.1613).

Varrius
A minor character in *Measure For Measure* (1604), who is an adherent of the Duke of Vienna.

Varrius
Minor character, a follower of Pompey in *Antony and Cleopatra* (1608).

Varro (Varrus)
A soldier in the army of Brutus following the murder of the title character in *Julius Caesar* (1599).

Varro's Servant
This walk-on could be either of two employees of Varro, who is a creditor of *Timon of Athens* (*c*.1604).

Vaughan, Sir Thomas
Minor historical figure who is an adherent of Queen Elizabeth in *Richard III* (*c*.1597). He speaks one line going to his death.

Vaux, Sir Nicholas
Minor courtier and historical figure in *Henry VIII* (1613).

Vaux, Sir William
A messenger in *Henry VI Part 2* (*c*.1594).

Venice, Duke of

The same as the traditional Doge of Venice, and usually so costumed in modern productions of *The Merchant of Venice* (c.1598) if the play is set in accurate period decor. He presides over the famous trial scene in which the ingenuity of Portia defeats Shylock. The Duke's role is small and ceremonial.

Venice, Duke of

This character is likewise the Doge, and functions only in an official capacity in *Othello* (1604).

Ventidius, Publius

Minor and historical figure in *Antony and Cleopatra* (1608), a subordinate of the hero.

Ventidius

One of the false friends of the hero in *Timon of Athens* (c.1604), a minor part.

Vergers

Two extras in *Henry VIII* (1613).

Verges

One of the comic nightwatchmen in *Much Ado About Nothing* (c.1599). Verges has little personality and his role is mainly to be a foil for Dogberry.

Vernon

A minor Yorkist follower in *Henry VI Part 1* (c.1592).

Vernon, Sir Richard

Minor historical figure, a follower of Hotspur in *Henry IV Part 1* (1598).

Vicentio

Minor character in *The Taming of The Shrew* (c.1594), an elderly man who is the father of Lucentio. They are part of the subplot of the wooing of Bianca.

Vincentio, Duke of Vienna

An important character in *Measure For Measure* (1604). At the beginning of the play the Duke goes into disguise as a Friar, leaving the stern Angelo to rule Vienna in his stead, but spying on his delegate. Fortunately the Duke is able to intervene just in time to prevent the consequences of Angelo's harsh justice. As a virtuous and religious man, the Duke is a suitable person for whom the heroine Isabella can renounce her intention to be a nun. By his rather abrupt decision to marry her, and his more moderate justice, the Duke acts as a divine agent, bringing all to a happy, or at least fair, conclusion. The role of the Duke is almost that of stage manager of the story.

Vintner

A bit part in the Boar's Head Tavern in *Henry IV Part 1* (1598), who contributes to the convivial atmosphere of an inn.

Viola

One of the most charming and resourceful of Shakespeare's heroines, found in *Twelfth Night* (1602). In terms of stage time, the role of Olivia in this comedy is about the same length, but Viola seems the more fully developed and interesting character. When we first meet her, she has endured the hardship of a shipwreck and separation from her twin brother, whom she thinks has drowned. Thrown on her own resources, she goes into disguise as a youth and becomes a page to the local grandee, Count Orsino,

Oscar Ashe as Vincentio, 1906.

with whom she instantly falls in love. She speaks of her love in veiled terms to him, as if she were speaking of an imaginary sister:

Orsino
And what's her history?
Viola
A blank, my lord. She never told her love,
But let concealment, like a worm i'th'bud,
Feed on her damask cheek. She pined in
   thought,
And with a green and yellow melancholy
She sat like Patience on a monument,
Smiling at grief. Was not this love indeed?

This famous passage is matched by another in which Viola again speaks of her love. In courting Olivia on the Duke's behalf, she is asked by the Countess how she would proceed.

Olivia
Why, what would you?
Viola
Make me a willow cabin at your gate
And call upon my soul within the house,
Write loyal cantons of contemned love,
And sing them loud even in the dead of night;
Halloo your name to the reverberate hills,
And make the babbling gossip of the air
Cry out 'Olivia!' O, you should not rest
Between the elements of air and earth
But you should pity me.

Although a very feminine character, Viola is able to act independently by virtue of her male disguise. The device of the breeches role was obviously a practical convenience in Shakespeare's theatre, where he was restricted to male actors, but it seems also to have freed the author's imagination to create a number of female roles whose character potential is expanded by this device. Notable among these are Viola, Portia, Imogen and Rosalind. Since they are characters in comedy, they are largely defined by personal relationships rather than public stances, with the exception of Portia. But their high intelligence, wit, and ability to act and take risks makes Shakespeare's comic heroines very modern women, generally much better able to cope with life than the male characters surrounding them. Viola has been played by many

Zoe Wanamaker plays Viola, 1983.

distinguished actresses, including Peg Woffington, Dora Jordan, Charlotte Cushman, Adelaide Neilson, Ellen Terry, Ada Rehan, Peggy Ashcroft, Vivien Leigh, Judi Dench and Zoe Wanamaker.

Virgilia
A small part, she is nevertheless the wife of the title figure in *Coriolanus* (1608) and the mother of his son. She is dominated by her heroic mother-in-law, Volumnia, who is by far the more important part. This helps to emphasize the abnormal influence which the mother has on her son.

Vision, The
Six silent female figures in *Henry VIII* (1613) they appear in a dream to Queen Katharine, who calls them 'spirits of peace'.

Volscians
Lords, citizens and senators who are members of this Italic tribe feature in *Coriolanus* (1608) as walk-ons and bit parts. The populace is important in this

play; the Volscians are enemies of Rome, and the hero appears in both camps in the course of his chequered career.

Voltimand
There are various spellings for this minor character in the several different early texts of *Hamlet* (*c*.1602); he is an ambassador from Denmark to Norway.

Volumnia
This mature Roman matron is one of the leading characters in *Coriolanus* (1608) and the mother of the title character. A widow and an aristocrat, she has raised her son to be a proud warrior to the exclusion of all else. She is domineering to an extreme and her moral code is warped. Volumnia is a legendary figure whom Shakespeare found in Plutarch's *Lives*, but he has greatly embellished her part in the story. Sarah Siddons, in the eighteenth century, gave a definitive performance of this difficult and unpleasant character.

Volumnius
Historical figure with a minor role in *Julius Caesar* (1599), Volumnius is a soldier in the army of Brutus.

W

Wales, Edward, Prince of
See Edward, Prince of Wales

Warders
Bit parts in *Henry VI Part 1* (*c*.1592), whose function is to man the Tower of London.

Wart, Thomas
One of Sir John Falstaff's recruits in *Henry IV Part 2* (1600), a rustic character.

Warwick, Richard Beauchamp, Earl of (1339?-1401?)
Historical character found in *Henry VI Part 1* (*c*.1592), *Henry V* (*c*.1599), and *Henry IV Part 2* (1600). He is a nobleman and distinguished warrior and is prominent in the Wars of the Roses.

Initially Warwick presents the Lancastrian King, Henry VI, with a petition supporting the restoration of his title to the Duke of York. Warwick is a party to the emblematic scene in the Temple Gardens, where noblemen pluck a white or a red rose to indicate which faction they support. Although Warwick picks a white rose, his stance in the play is conciliatory. Gradually the importance of Warwick as a stage character diminishes. In the other two 'Henry' plays Warwick is a younger figure, an advisor to Henry IV who defends the young Prince Hal against his father's disapproval. In *Henry V* Warwick speaks only one line. The historical character was far more important than he is in the three plays.

Warwick, Richard Neville, Earl of (1428-71)
This bold nobleman and warrior was also a historical figure active in the Wars of the Roses. His character appears in *Henry VI Parts 2 and 3* (*c*.1594/*c*.1595), and he is the son-in-law of the earlier Warwick. It is Neville who was known after his death as 'the kingmaker'. He supports the Yorkist side initially and Edward IV is his protégé, but when the King abruptly turns away from a marriage arrangement made by Warwick on his behalf with a French princess and marries the commoner, Lady Elizabeth Woodville Grey, he loses the support of his advocate. Warwick changes his allegiance to the Lancastrians, King Henry VI and Queen Margaret, but seems to have been genuinely patriotic, and not as fickle as Shakespeare has made him, due to the necessity of telescoping stage time. Warwick remains in the background of events, as his two daughters marry the younger brothers of King Edward IV. He dies in battle.

Watchman
Patrols who are found in *Henry VI Part 3* (*c*.1595), *Romeo and Juliet* (1597), *Much Ado About Nothing* (*c*.1599), *Antony and Cleopatra* (1608), and *Coriolanus* (1608).

Normally watchmen, who can be of various ages, function in night scenes. They are working class characters, sometimes humorous.

Westmoreland, Richard Neville, Earl of
Historical figure found in *Henry IV Parts 1 and 2* (1598/1600) and *Henry V* (*c*.1599), a loyal councillor to Henry IV, although his character is sketchy. In *Henry V* his role is even less important, but Shakespeare erroneously depicts him as a participant at the Battle of Agincourt.

Westmoreland, Ralph Neville, Earl of
Historical character, the grandson of the above and a minor character in *Henry VI Part 3* (*c*.1595). He is depicted as a Lancastrian adherent although the real man was not a participant in the Wars of the Roses.

Whitmore, Walter
This very minor character may have been historical. He is a pirate in *Henry VI Part 2* (*c*.1594) who executes the Duke of Suffolk, the lover of Queen Margaret.

Widow
A bit part who appears in the final banquet scene in *The Taming of the Shrew* (*c*.1594) as one of three brides. Her role is undeveloped and her function is merely to act as one more female witness to Katherina's newly obedient demeanour as a wife and tamed shrew.

Widow Capilet
Minor character, a landlady in *All's Well That Ends Well* (*c*.1603).

Wife
A walk-on who is the spouse of a villager, one Simpcox, found in *Henry VI Part 2* (*c*.1594).

William
This young rustic swain is an inhabitant of the Forest of Arden in *As You Like It* (1600). William is a caricature of a peasant and he loses Audrey, a shepherdess, to Touchstone, a more sophisticated lover.

Williams, Michael
One of several small roles which are nevertheless so well delineated by Shakespeare as soldiers of the English King in *Henry V* (*c*.1599). They represent a cross-section of types and attitudes in the 'band of brothers' who were so heavily out-numbered at the Battle of Agincourt. Williams holds a debate with the disguised King on the eve of the battle, which is a very telling episode.

Willoughby, William de
Minor character in *Richard II* (1597), a follower of Henry Bolingbroke.

Winchester, Henry Beaufort
See Beaufort, Cardinal.

Winchester, Stephen Gardiner, Bishop of
See Gardiner.

Witches
These three very famous figures are found in *Macbeth* (1606); they form a chorus and at times speak in unison. As they are supernatural creatures, the witches are open to considerable interpretation. On separate occasions, the playwright implies that they are variously male and female. They are clearly ugly, although Holinshed's *Chronicles* refers to fairies and nymphs appearing to Macbeth, which would imply beauty; the author presumably departed from his source as

The Three Witches, by Henry Fuseli.

he wished the witches to personify evil. Whether one accepts them realistically, as Shakespeare's own age did, or takes the modern view of them, as manifestations of the darker side of human nature, they are unquestionably a powerful poetic metaphor. The subject of 'Macbeth and the Witches' is a frequent one in art.

Wolsey, Cardinal Thomas (1475?-1530)

This major historical character is one of the outstanding roles in the canon, although we must remember that *Henry VIII* (1613) is credited to both Shakespeare and Fletcher. Cardinal Wolsey is both physically large and metaphorically larger than life. He is an over-powerful advisor to the King and his machinations are machiavellian; he is the enemy of the play's pristine heroine, Queen Katharine. Once his wrong-doings are uncovered, the fall of Wolsey proceeds in true tragic fashion, as he comes to recognise that he has disgraced his priestly calling in his pursuit of power and wealth. He befriends Thomas Cromwell and makes his peace with God. In his final scenes, Wolsey has some magnificent dialogue, which culminates:

> . . . O Cromwell, Cromwell,
> Had I but served my God with half the zeal
> I served my King, He would not in mine age
> Have left me naked to mine enemies.

ABOVE Cardinal Wolsey with Henry VIII, by C. Walter Hodges.
BELOW LEFT Henry Irving as Cardinal Wolsey.

Woman
Any of several walk-ons who are servants to Queen Katharine in *Henry VIII* (1613) are called 'woman'. One sings a song to cheer her.

Woman
A minor attendant on Emilia in *The Two Noble Kinsmen* (c.1613).

Woodville
See Rivers.

Woodville
See Elizabeth, Queen of England.

Woodville (Woodvile), Lieutenant Richard
Minor historical figure who was the father of the future Queen Elizabeth, but within the context of *Henry VI Part 1* (c.1592), he is merely the commander of the warders at the Tower of London.

Wooer
This bit part is suitor of the gaoler's daughter in *The Two Noble Kinsmen* (c.1613).

Worcester, Thomas Percy, Earl of
This historical figure plays a marginal part in *Henry IV Part 1* (1598). He is the uncle of Hotspur, leader of the rebels against the King, and a sinister figure.

Y

York, Cecily Neville, Duchess of (1415-1495)

An important historical character in *Richard III* (*c*.1597), she is of very advanced years. The title 'Queen Mother' was not used in those days, but the Duchess is the mother of two Kings, Edward IV and the brother who succeeded him, Richard III, as well as of the murdered Duke of Clarence. The Duchess is important in that she laments the evil of Richard, her own son, and ends by cursing him. At one point, she functions as a tragic chorus, together with Queen Margaret and Queen Elizabeth, in the so-called 'weeping queens' scene, in another of those emblematic moments found in the histories.

York, Isabel of Castile, Duchess of

Historical but minor figure in *Richard II* (*c*.1597), who is the mother of the Duke of Aumerle, a plotter against the new King, Henry IV.

York, Edmund Langley, Duke of

The uncle of the title figure in *Richard II* (1597) and the elderly husband of Isabel, Duchess of York. The Duke is such a sound supporter of kingship that he even gives up his son, Aumerle, when the latter turns traitor. York is a gentle and honourable old man, and is representative of traditional values, but is ineffective in the public arena.

York, Edward, Duke of

See Aumerle.

York, Richard, Duke of

The younger of the so-called 'princes in the Tower'. His murder, and that of his elder brother, the uncrowned King Edward V, is tragic and poignant, and a pivotal episode (offstage) in *Richard III* (*c*.1597).

York, Richard Plantagenet, Duke of (1411-60)

Anton Lesser as Richard, Duke of York, 1978.

This major historical figure is a warrior in the Wars of the Roses and an important character throughout the trilogy of *Henry VI* (*c*.1592-*c*.1595). He is the claimant to the throne on the Yorkist side, and although he does not personally achieve his objective, he is the father of two kings, Edward IV and Richard III. The Duke of York is ruthlessly ambitious, and promotes the rebellion of Jack Cade against King Henry. In the final part of the trilogy, he has a dramatic death scene in which he confronts Queen Margaret, whose captive he is, but he remains a one-dimensional character.

York, Archbishop of, Thomas Rotherham

See Rotherham.

York, Archbishop of, Richard Scroop

See Scroop.

Young Lucius

Minor character, grandson of the title character in *Titus Andronicus* (*c*.1594).

Young Macduff

See Son.

Young Siward

Minor character, the son of Siward, Earl of Northumberland, in *Macbeth* (1606).

Young Martius

This virtually silent figure is the son of the title character in Coriolanus (1608).

Acknowledgements

The publisher would like to thank Ron Callow of Design 23 for designing this book; Suzanne O'Farrell, with Rita Longabucco, for picture research; Simon Shelmerdine, production manager; and Jessica Hodge, editor. We should also like to thank the following individuals, institutions and agencies for permission to reproduce photographic material.

The Bettmann Archive: pages 2 (top right), 20, 43, 65 (bottom right), 74, 150 (bottom).
Brompton Picture Library: page 65 (top).
Donald Cooper/Photostage: pages 2 (bottom left and right), 7 (bottom), 13, 15, 16/17, 18, 22 (top), 25, 26/27, 27, 29 (both), 30, 34 (bottom), 37 (bottom), 38 (bottom), 40, 45 (bottom), 47, 50, 52/53, 54, 57 (top), 62 (both), 69, 70, 76, 77 (both), 79 (top), 83, 84, 85 (top), 86, 87, 88 (bottom), 89, 94, 95, 98/99, 101, 103 (top), 104/105, 105, 109 (bottom), 112 (both), 114/115, 116, 117 (both), 119, 121, 122/123, 125 (top), 127 (both), 129, 131, 134 (bottom), 136, 141 (top), 147, 148 (both), 150 (top), 151, 152, 155, 159.
Devonshire Collection, Chatsworth. Reproduced by permission of the Chatsworth Settlement Tr   page 9.
C. Walter Hodges: pages   , 7 (top), 32 (top), 35 (top), 48, 51 (top), 64, 67, 125 (bottom), 146, 158 (top).
Hulton Deutsch Collection Ltd: pages 12, 14, 17, 21, 22 (bottom), 24, 28, 31, 37 (top), 38 (top), 41, 42, 44 (top), 46, 49, 51 (bottom), 55, 57 (bottom), 58, 59, 60, 61, 65 (bottom right), 66, 68, 71, 72, 73, 75, 78, 79 (bottom), 80 (bottom), 88 (top), 91, 92 (bottom), 93, 96 (both), 98 (top), 99, 102, 103 (bottom), 106, 107, 108, 109 (top), 110, 111, 113, 115, 120, 123, 128, 130, 133, 138, 139, 140, 141 (bottom), 142, 143, 144, 145, 154, 157, 159 (bottom).
Courtesy of the International Shakespeare Globe Centre: page 6.
Reproduced by permission of the Marquess of Bath, Longleat House, Warminster, Wilts: page 10.
National Portrait Gallery, London: page 1.
Courtesy of Dr Wendy Nelson-Cave: pages 2 (top right), 20, 43, 74, 150 (bottom).
Springer/Bettmann Film Archive: pages 32 (bottom), 80 (top), 82, 90, 92 (top), 118, 126, 134 (top), 135 (top).